RECORDED VERSIONS
GUITAR

AUTHENTIC TRANSCRIPTIONS
WITH NOTES AND TABLATURE

THE ROLLING STONES
GUITAR ANTHOLOGY

Front cover photo by Dimo Safari/CORBIS SYGMA

ISBN 0-634-06286-7

HAL•LEONARD®
CORPORATION

7777 W. BLUEMOUND RD. P.O. BOX 13819 MILWAUKEE, WI 53213

Visit Hal Leonard Online at
www.halleonard.com

All the Way Down

Words and Music by Mick Jagger and Keith Richards

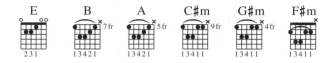

* Producer Chris Kimsey

** Chord symbols reflect overall tonality.

Her wit, her speech,__ her rep-ar-tee __ im-pressed me al-most in-stant-ly. __

mf w/ clean tone

Chorus

(Oh!)   (She ran   all the way,   all the way __ down.

hold bend
full

1/4

* = low strs. only (throughout).

Bridge
Half-Time Feel

there when I close my eyes, there when I close my eyes.

She's there when I close my eyes, there when I close my eyes.

let ring

let ring

let ring

4. How the years rush on by: birth-days, kids,_ and

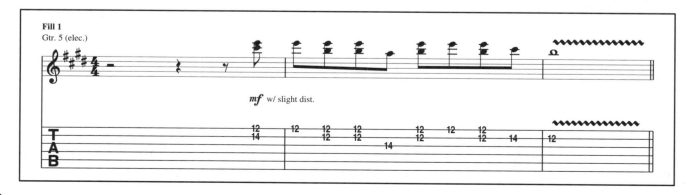

She ran all the way, all the way, all the way, all the way

down. (All the way.)

She ran all the way, all the way, all the way, all the way)

18

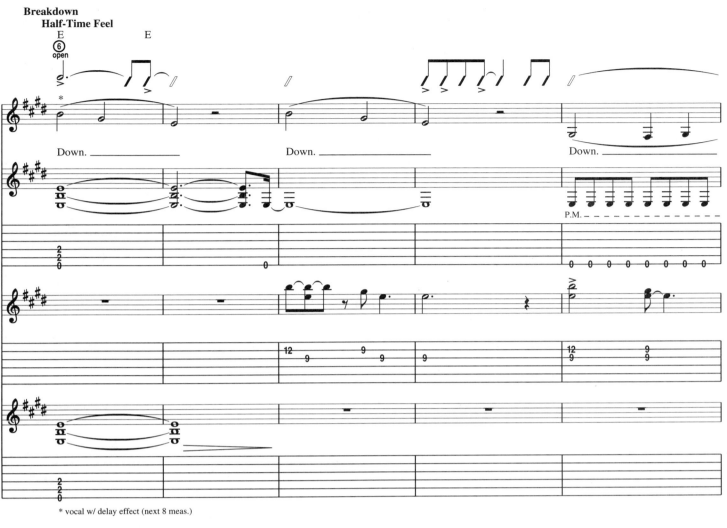

* vocal w/ delay effect (next 8 meas.)

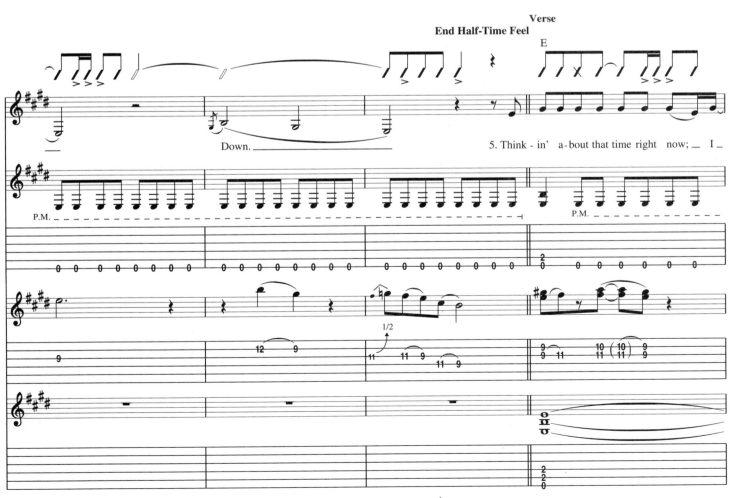

19

All the way _____ down. _____ She ran all the way,
all the way down. _____ She ran all the way, all the way, _

all the way _ down. _____ She ran all the way, _____
all the way _ down. _____ She ran all the way, all the way, _

all the way   down. _____   Now,   she   ran
all the way   down.   She   ran

all the way,   all the way,   all the way,   all the way _____   down.
all the way,   all the way,   all the way,   all the way __   down. _____

Begin Fade

Angie

Words and Music by Mick Jagger and Keith Richards

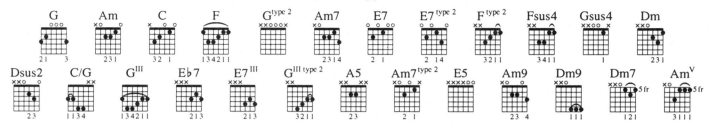

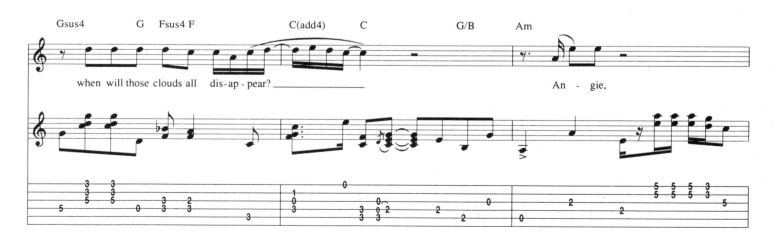

Lyrics: An - gie, where will it lead us from here! ___

(Oh!)

*Gtr. 3 w/ pick and fingers

*Piano arr. for gtr.
**Violin arr. for gtr.
***Simulate bowing w/vol. pedal throughout.

Beast of Burden

Words and Music by Mick Jagger and Keith Richards

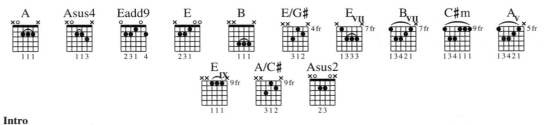

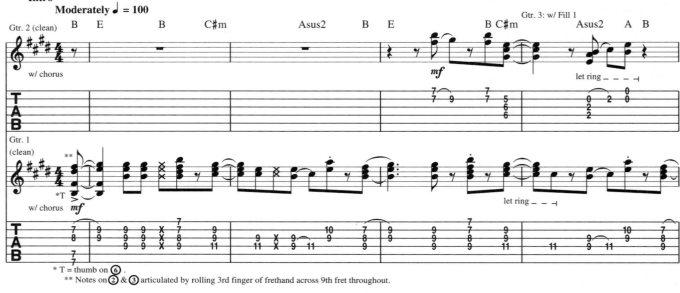

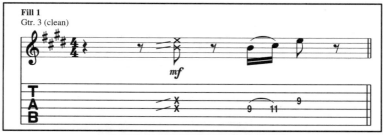

1. I'll nev-er be __ your beast __ of bur-den. My back is broad, __ but it's a hurt-in'.

All I want for you to make a love to me. _____

Chorus

hard e-nough? Am I rough e-nough? Am I rich e-nough? I'm not too blind __ to see...

** Gtr. 3 tabbed to left of slash.   *** Gtr. 6 tabbed to left of slash.

* Gtr. 4 is a Nashville-tuned acous.: strs. ③ through ⑥
are tuned one octave higher than normal.

Verse

3. I'll nev-er be ___ your beast of bur-den so let's go home ___

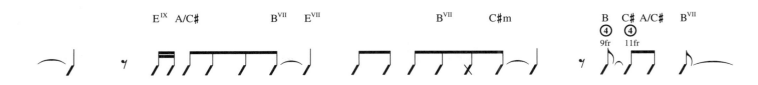

Chorus

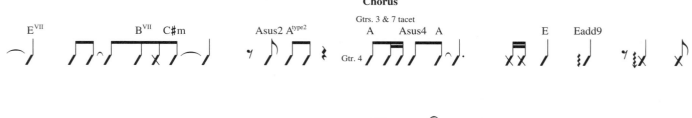

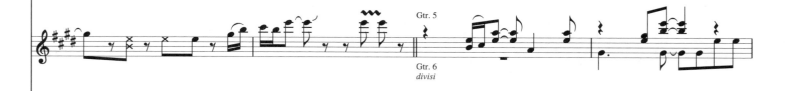

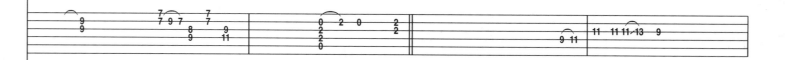

rich e - nough?   I'm not too blind __ to see. __

Guitar Solo

Gtrs. 4, 5 & 6 tacet

Oh, _____ lit - tle sis - ter. _____ Pret - ty, pret - ty, pret - ty, pret - ty girls. _____

* Release finger pressure and slide.

let ring _ _ _ _ _ _ T

Come on, ___ ba - by, please, ___ please, ___ please. ___

4. I tell ya, you can
(Spoken: Wanna tell ya somethin'...)

Verse

put me out on the street, put me out with no ___ shoes ___

rough e-nough? Oo, ____ hon-ey. Ain't I tough e-nough?
(Oo, ____ hon-ey.)

Ain't I rich e-nough? In love e-nough? Oo oo, ____ please.

* Release finger pressure and slide to 9th fret.

I'll nev - er be ___ your

beast of bur - den. I'll nev - er be ___ your beast of bur - den.

Nev - er, nev - er, nev - er, nev - er, nev - er nev - er, nev - er be.

Shh.   (Inhale)   I'll nev - er be   your beast   of bur - den.

I've walked for miles, ___ my feet are hurt - in', uh. Well, all I want ___ is

you to make love to me. ___ uh. Yeah. ___ (Inhale)

50

Black Limousine

Words and Music by Mick Jagger, Keith Richards and Ron Wood

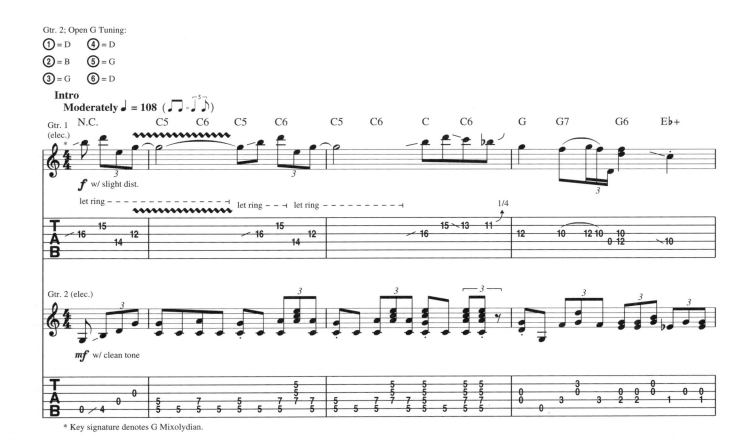

* Key signature denotes G Mixolydian.

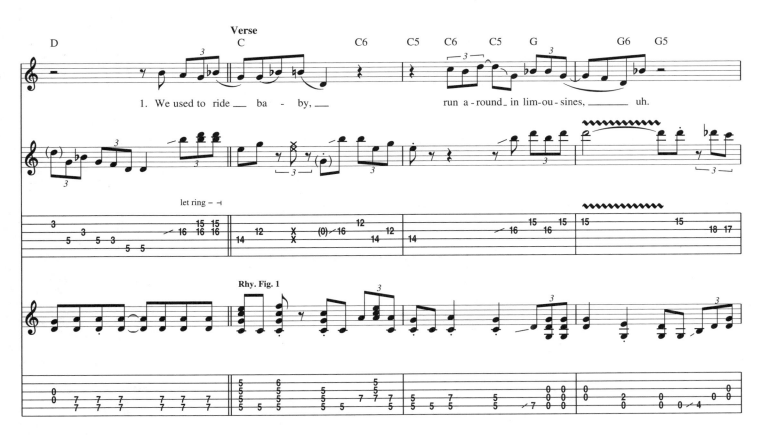

3. We used to shine,

57

Verse

look at you, __ look at me. _____ Look out! Whoa, yeah.

Outro Solo
Gtr. 2: w/ Rhy. Fig. 2, simile

Begin Fade
Gtr. 2: w/ Rhy. Fig. 2, first 7 meas., simile

Fade Out

Doo Doo Doo Doo Doo (Heartbreaker)

Words and Music by Mick Jagger and Keith Richards

Verse

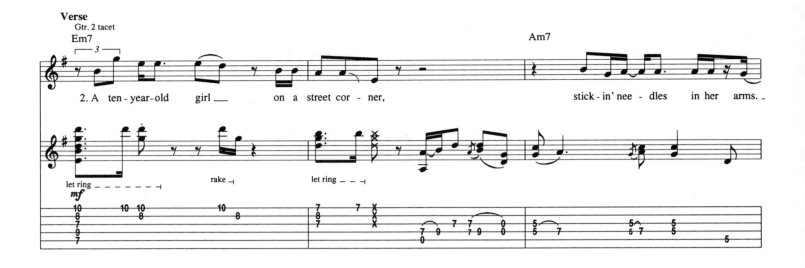

2. A ten-year-old girl __ on a street cor-ner, stick-in' nee-dles in her arms. __

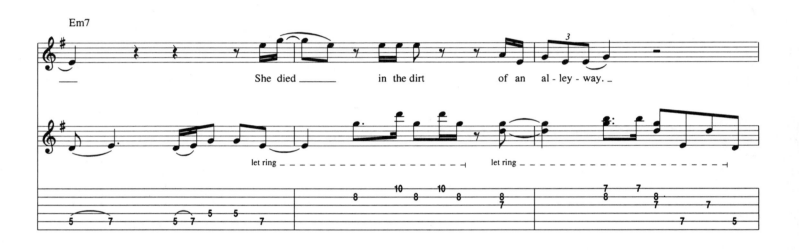

She died _____ in the dirt of an al-ley-way. __

Chorus

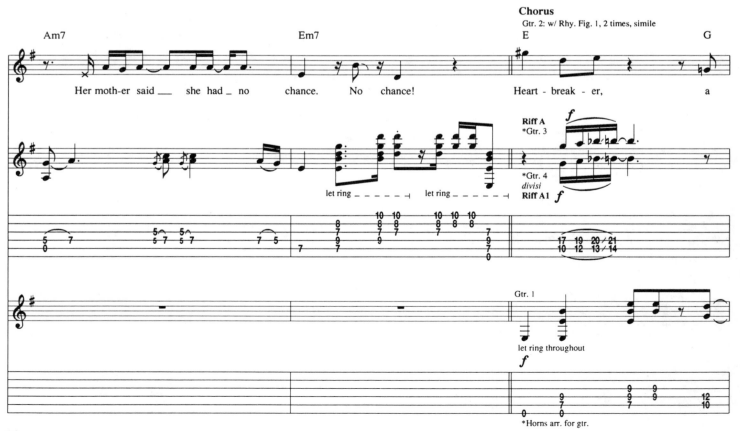

Her moth-er said __ she had _ no chance. No chance! Heart-break-er, a

*Horns arr. for gtr.

G5   C5

part. __   Oh,   yeah! _____   Oh, _____ yeah! __
doo.   Doo,   doo doo doo   doo doo doo,   doo doo   doo   doo doo

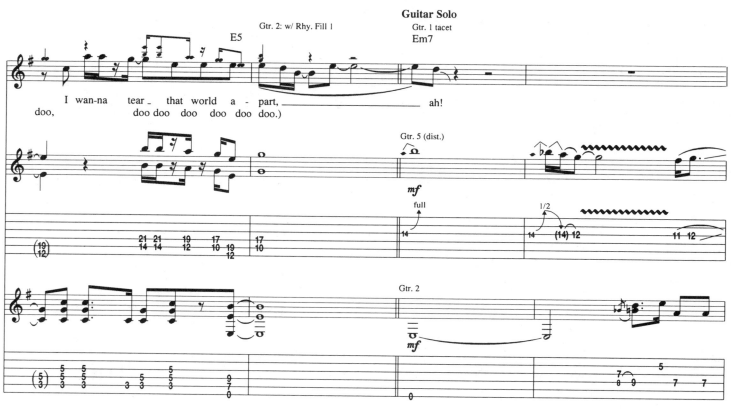

Guitar Solo

Gtr. 2: w/ Rhy. Fill 1   Gtr. 1 tacet
E5   Em7

I wan-na tear __ that world a-part, _____ ah!
doo,   doo doo doo doo doo doo.)

Gtr. 5 (dist.)

Gtr. 2

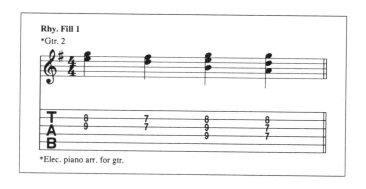

Rhy. Fill 1
*Gtr. 2

*Elec. piano arr. for gtr.

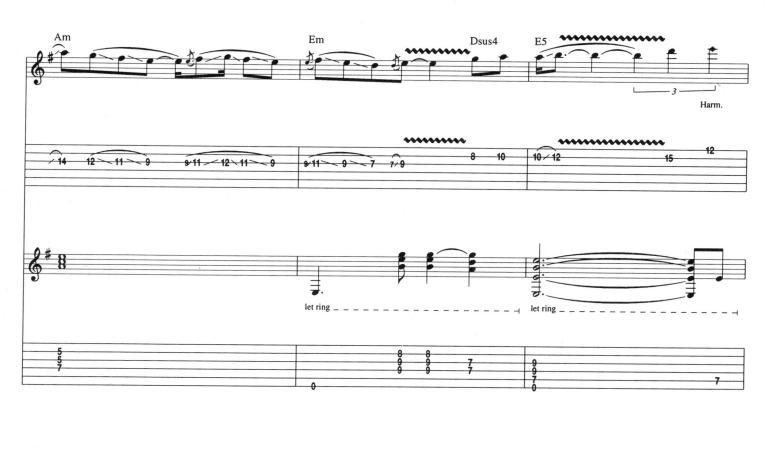

Chorus

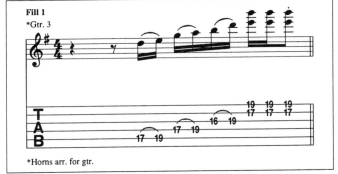

*Horns arr. for gtr.

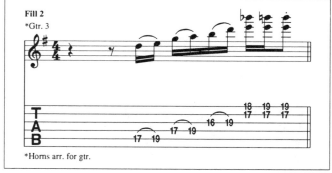

69

Emotional Rescue

Words and Music by Mick Jagger and Keith Richards

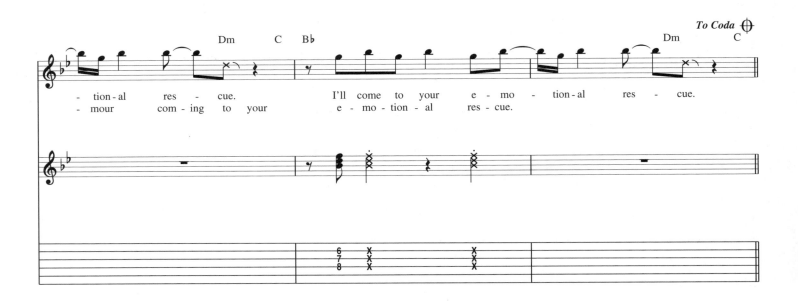

Yes, _____ I'm like a child, like a child, _ like a child, _ like a child. _

let ring -

Verse

Gtr. 1: w/ Rhy. Fig. 2, 3 1/2 times
Gtr. 2: w/ Rhy. Fig. 3, 7 times

Gtrs. 1 & 2: w/ Rhy. Fills 1 & 2

Woo.
3. You think you're one of a spe-cial breed, _

you think that you're re-spect me please. _ I'll be your sav-ior, stead-fast and true.

Gtr. 1 tacet

I'll come to your e - mo - tion - al res - cue. I'll come to your e - mo - tion - al res - cue.

Rhy. Fill 1
Gtr. 1

Rhy. Fill 2
Gtr. 2

74

D.S. al Coda

⊕ **Coda**

Outro

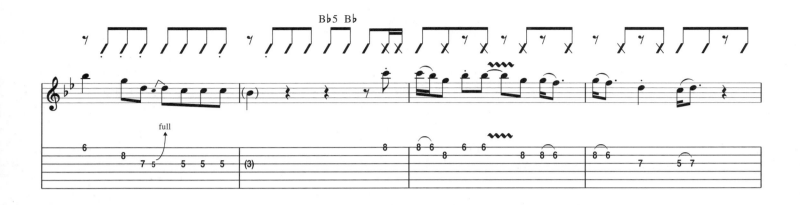

Gtr. 3: w/ Rhy. Fig. 6, 9 times, simile

Rhy. Fig. 6   **End Rhy. Fig. 6**

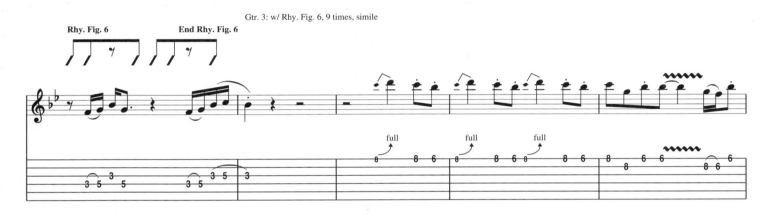

Gtr. 3: w/ Rhy. Fill 3,
1st meas., 3 times, simile

Begin Fade

Gtr. 3: w/ Rhy. Fig. 6, 9 times, simile

Fade Out

77

Fool to Cry

Words and Music by Mick Jagger and Keith Richards

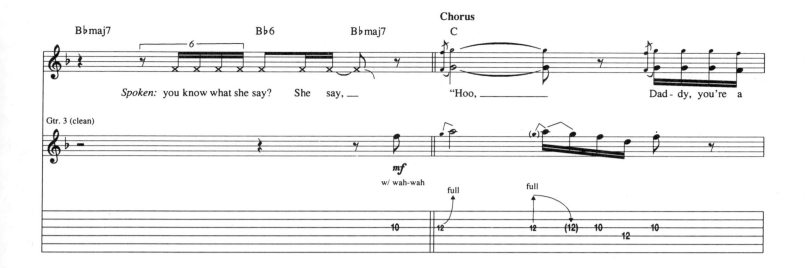

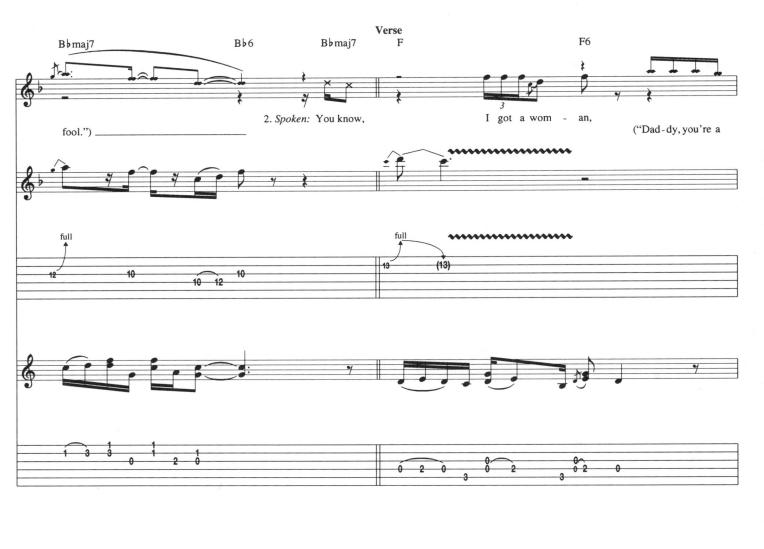

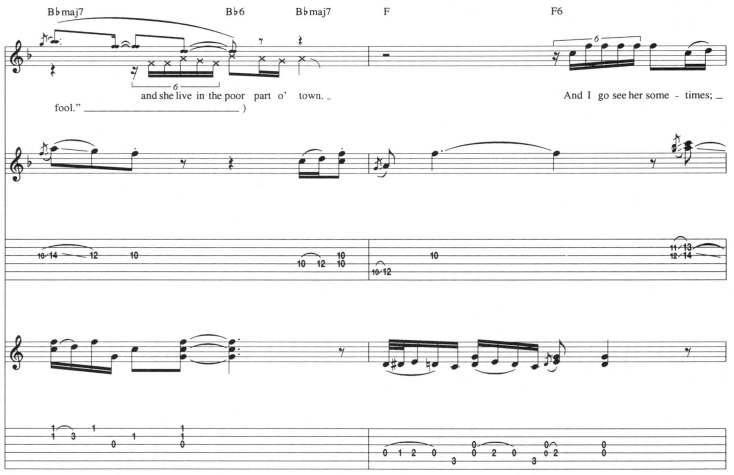

we make love _ so _ fine.

I put my head on her shoul-der.

Riff B

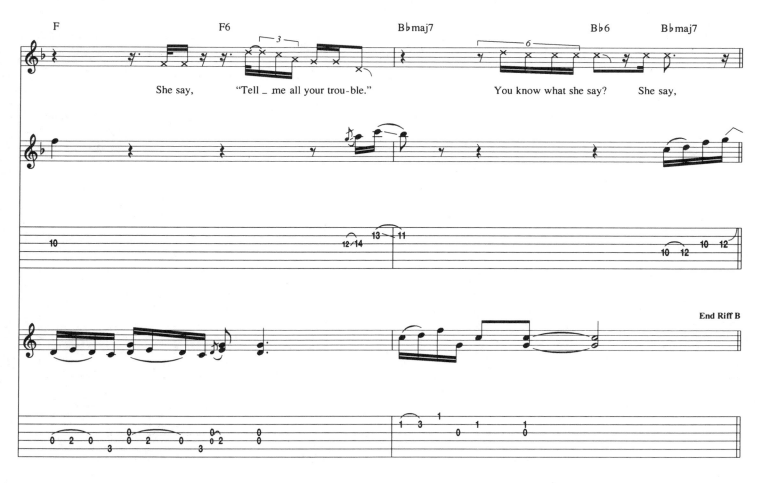

She say, "Tell _ me all your trou-ble."

You know what she say? She say,

End Riff B

fool   to cry. _____   Oo   hoo, _____   dad-dy, you're a   fool   to cry. _____

Oo   hoo, _____   dad-dy, you're a   fool   to cry.   Oo   hoo, _____   dad-dy, you're a

Verse
Gtr. 4: w/ Riff B, simile

fool   to cry." _____   3. *Spoken:* E - ven my   friends   say to me

Hang Fire

Words and Music by Mick Jagger and Keith Richards

Intro

Moderately Fast ♩ = 152

* C# played by bass.

Happy

Words and Music by Mick Jagger and Keith Richards

Gtrs. 1 & 2: Open G Tuning, Capo IV

① = D	④ = D
② = B	⑤ = G
③ = G	⑥ = D

Gtr. 3; Open D Tuning

① = D	④ = D
② = A	⑤ = A
③ = F#	⑥ = D

Intro

♩ = 130

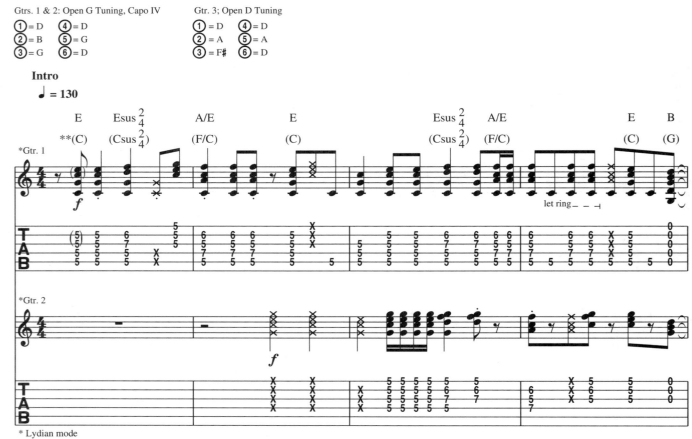

* Lydian mode

** Symbols in parenthesis represent chord names respective to capoed guitar.
Symbols above reflect actual sounding of chord.

1. Well, I nev-

* Two gtrs. arr. for one.

Verse

-er kept a dol-lar past sun - set; al - ways burned a hole in my pants._____ Nev-

Rhy. Fig. 2

w/o slide

w/ slide _ _ _ _ _

-er made a school ma-ma hap - py; nev - er blew a sec-ond chance _ on love. _

End Rhy. Fig. 2

w/o slide

w/ slide

let ring

Coda 1

Guitar Solo
Gtrs. 1 & 2: w/ Rhy. Figs. 1 & 1A

*Gtr. 3

* Mixolydian mode

Pre-Chorus
Gtrs. 1 & 2: w/ Rhy. Fills 1 & 2
Gtrs. 1 & 2: w/ Rhy. Figs. 3 & 3A, simile
Gtr. 3 tacet

Rhy. Fill 1
Gtr. 1

Rhy. Fill 2
Gtr. 2

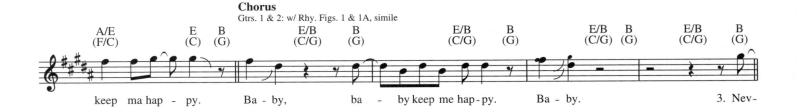

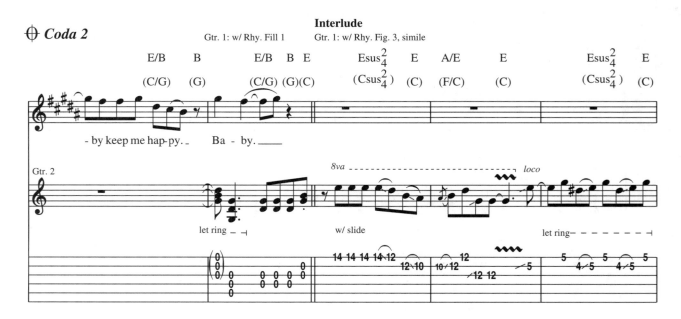

The Harlem Shuffle

Written by Bob Relf and Earl Nelson

* Chord symbols reflect overall tonality.

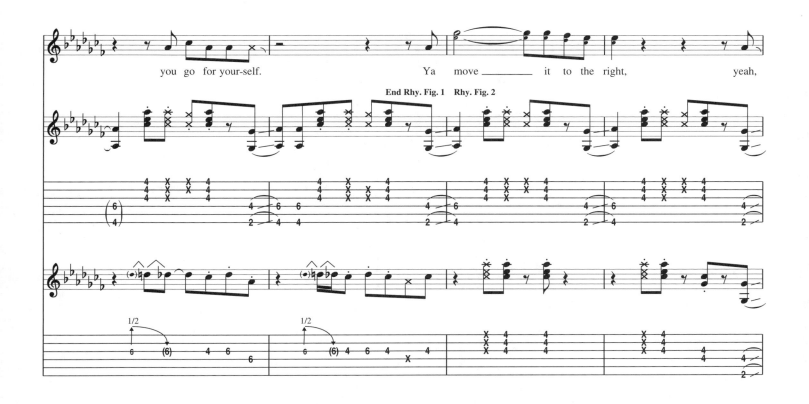

you go for your-self.   Ya move _____ it to the right,   yeah,

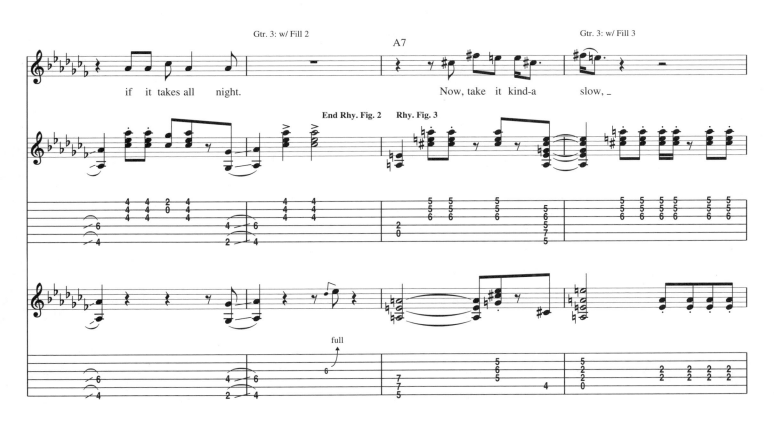

if it takes all night.   Now, take it kind-a slow, __

with a whole lot o' soul. _____ And don't move _____ it too fast, just make it last. _ 2. Ya

Gtr. 1: w/ Rhy. Fig. 2, 1st 2 meas., simile

Ab m

Ah. _____

Ah. _____

let ring

Verse

Gtr. 4 tacet
Am

3. Hitch, hitch-hike ba-by, a-cross the floor.

Gtr. 3

Gtr. 1

Gtr. 2

110

Whoa, whoa, whoa,

I can't stand it no more.

Now, come on ba -

- by. _____ (Yeah, come on ba - by now.)   Get in - to your slide. _____   Just

End Rhy. Fig. 5

Gtr. 1: w/ Rhy. Fig. 4, simile

Am

ride, ride, _ ride, lit - tle po - ny ride. _____

Gtr. 3

Gtr. 2

Chorus

113

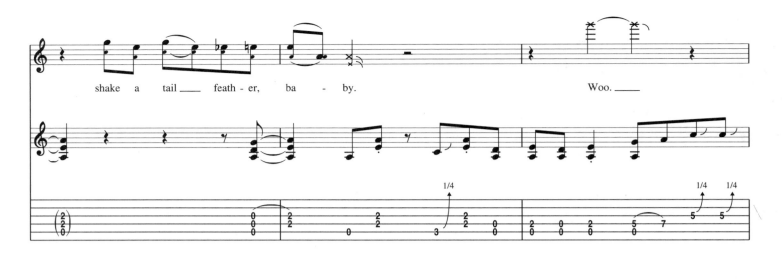

shake a tail ___ feath- er, ba - by. Woo. ___

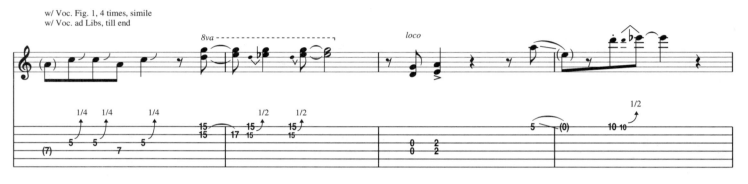

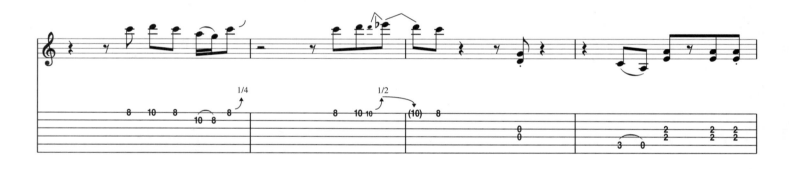

It's Only Rock 'n' Roll
(But I Like It)

Words and Music by Mick Jagger and Keith Richards

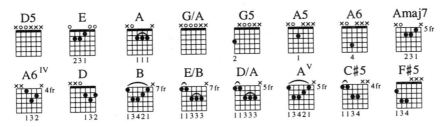

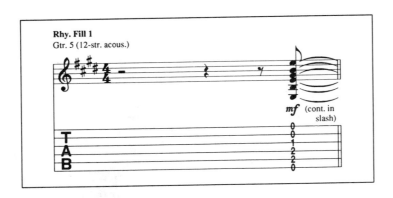

If ___ I could win ___ ya, if ___ I could sing ___ ya a love song so di - vine,___

would ___ it be e - nough for your cheat - in' heart ___ if ___

118

I said, I know __ it's on-ly rock 'n' roll, but I

like it.   I   like   it. _____   I   said,

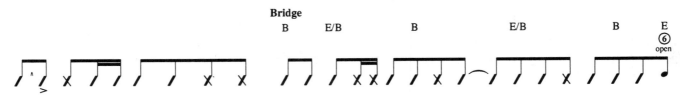

Mm.   And do you think that you're the on - ly girl   a - round?

you're the on-ly wom-an in town, _____ uh! Oo! Yeah!

like it. ___ Oo yeah! ___ I like it. ___ Oo yeah! ___ I
(On - ly rock 'n' roll, but ...) (On - ly rock 'n' roll, but ...)

like it, ___ Oo, yeah! ___ I like it. ___ Oo yeah. ___ I
(On - ly rock 'n' roll, but ...) (On - ly rock 'n' roll, but ...)

Rhy. Fig. 4
Gtr. 3

Miss You

Words and Music by Mick Jagger and Keith Richards

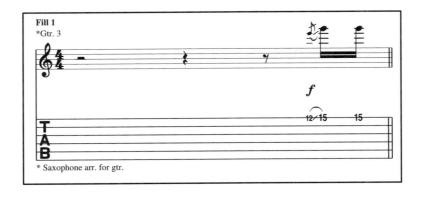

Fill 1
*Gtr. 3

* Saxophone arr. for gtr.

3. I guess, I'm ly - in' to my - self, __ it's just you.

*Harmonica arr. for gtr.

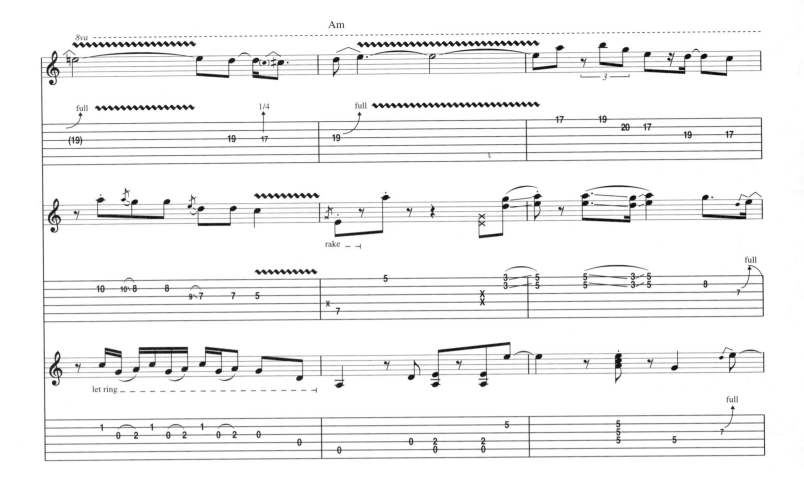

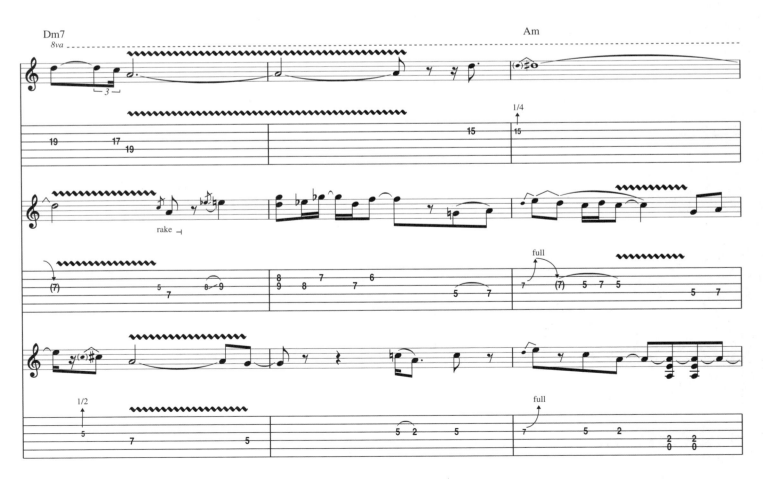

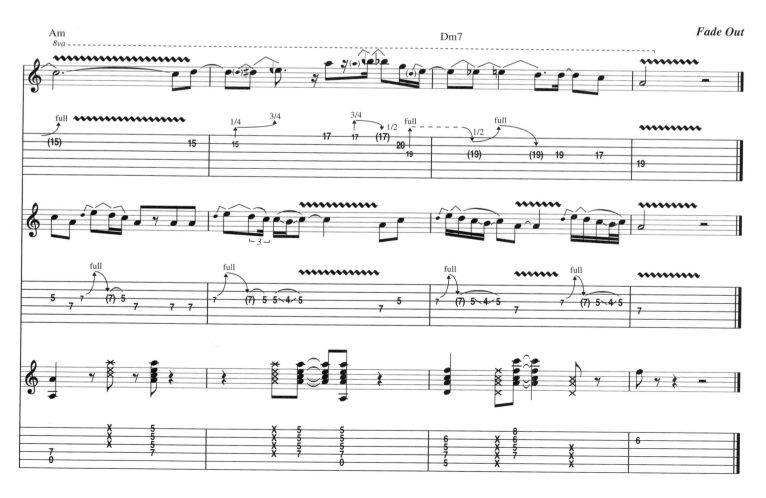

Not Fade Away

Words and Music by Charles Hardin and Norman Petty

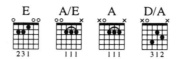

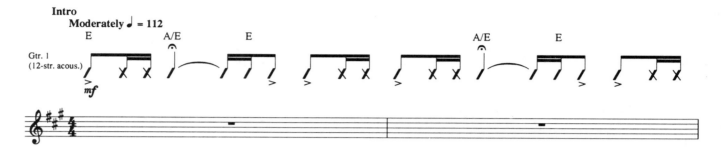

1. I wan-na tell ya how it's _ gon - na be.

Uh, you're gon-na give your love to me.

I'm gon-na love you night. and day. _ Oh, love is love, _ not fade a - way. _

Uh, well, love is love, _ not fade a - way. _ 2. Uh,

Verse

my love's big - ger than a Cad - il - lac. _ I _ try to show it and you drive me back. _

Uh, your love for me has got _ to be real, _

for you to know just how I feel. Uh, love real, _ not fade a - way. _

Chorus

Uh, well, love real, _ not fade a - way. _ Yeah!

Interlude

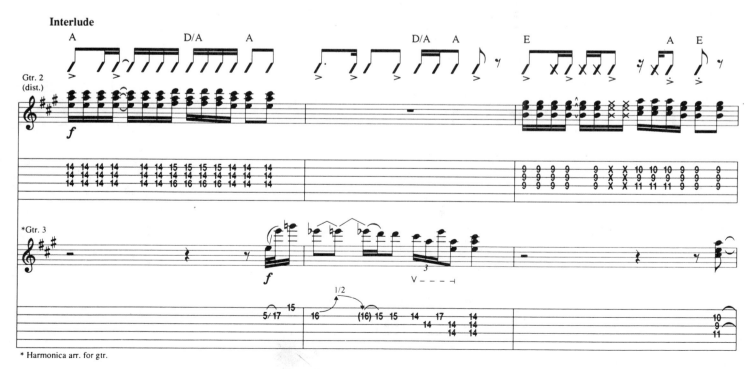

* Harmonica arr. for gtr.

151

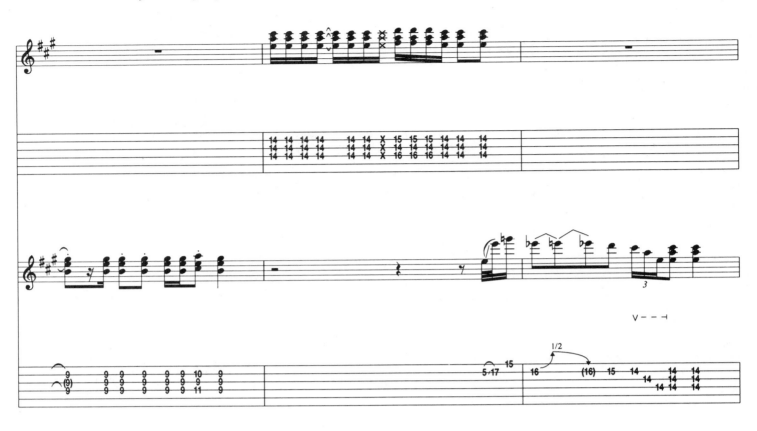

Verse
Gtrs. 2 & 3 tacet

3. I'm gon-na tell ya how it's ___ gon - na be. ___ Uh _

your gon-na give your love to me. A love that lasts _ more than one day. _

Chorus

Uh well, love is love, ___ not fade a-way. ___ Well,

Outro

love is love, ___ not fade a-way. ___ Well, love is love, _ not fade a-way. _____

Begin Fade

L - love, love, 'll not fade a-way. ___ Not
(Love, love, _ not fade a-way.) ___ (Not

Fade Out

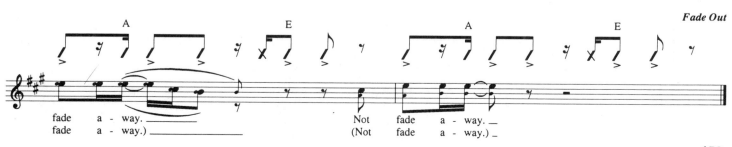

fade a - way. Not fade a-way. _
fade a - way.) _____ (Not fade a-way.) _

Respectable

Words and Music by Mick Jagger and Keith Richards

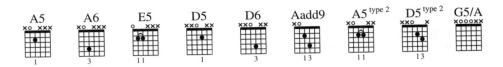

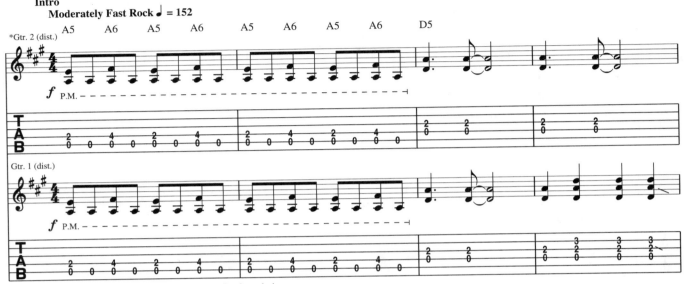

*Gtr. 2 is a Telecaster fitted with a Parsons-White B string Bender, a device
which enables Ron Wood to bend the B string by pulling on the guitar's neck.

- ta my life, ___   don't come back. ___   Get out-

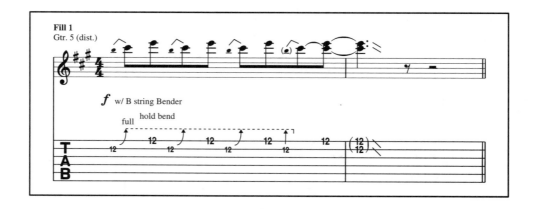

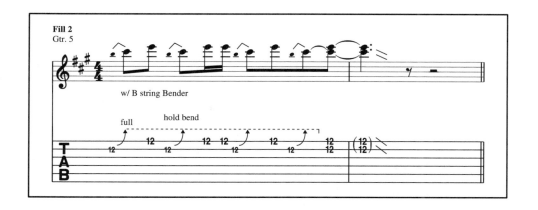

Chorus

* Release finger pressure to produce harmonic
which rings from sympathetic string.

go take my wife, _ don't come back! _   I   say! _____

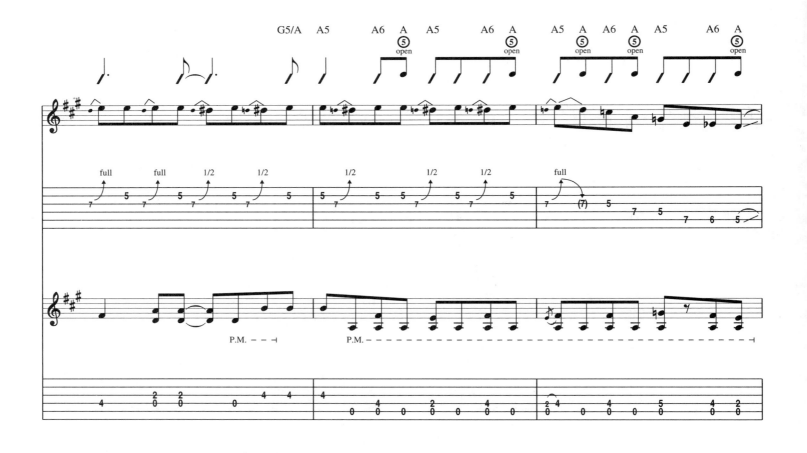

She's so re-

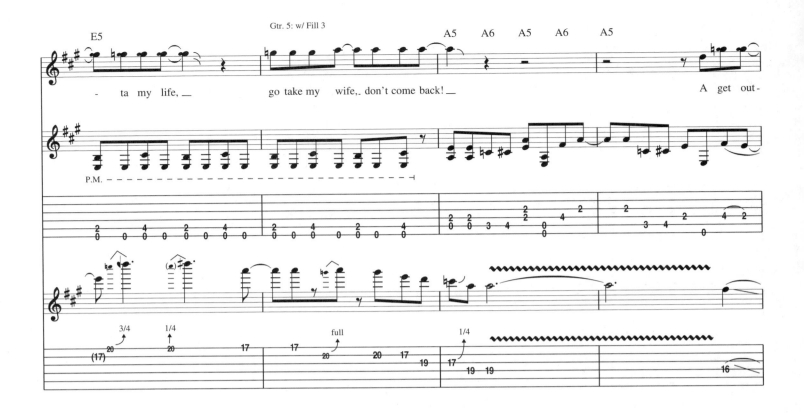

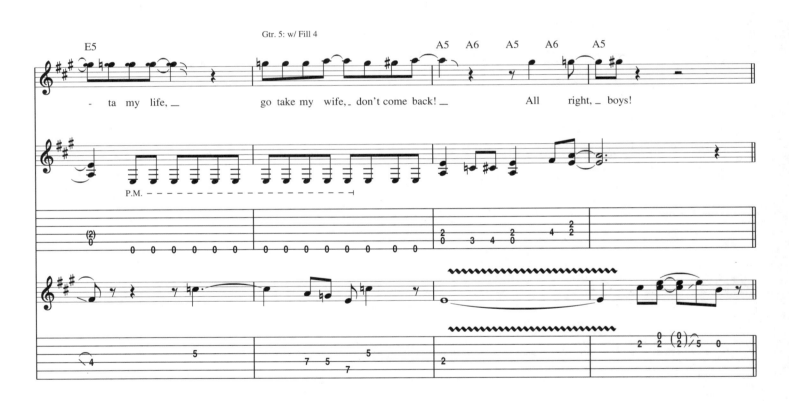

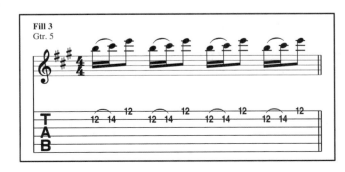

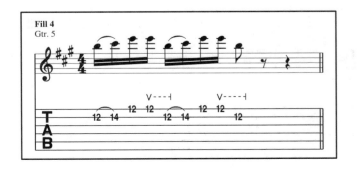

Guitar Solo

Gtr. 3: w/ Rhy. Fig. 2, simile
Gtr. 4: w/ Rhy. Fig. 1A, 1st 12 meas., simile

* Microphone fdbk., not caused by string vibration.
** Vib. A (③ 14 fr) only, just enough to make the
note sound slightly out of tune.

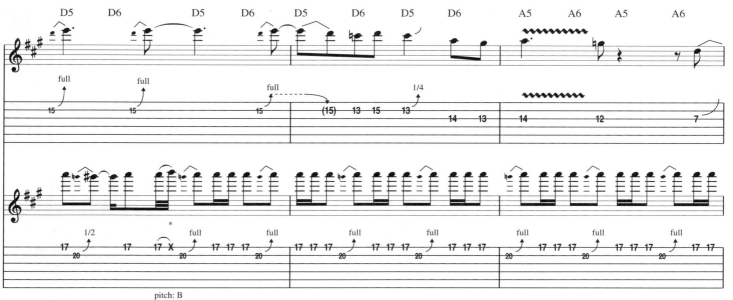

pitch: B
* Note is sounded by pulling str. off side of fretboard.

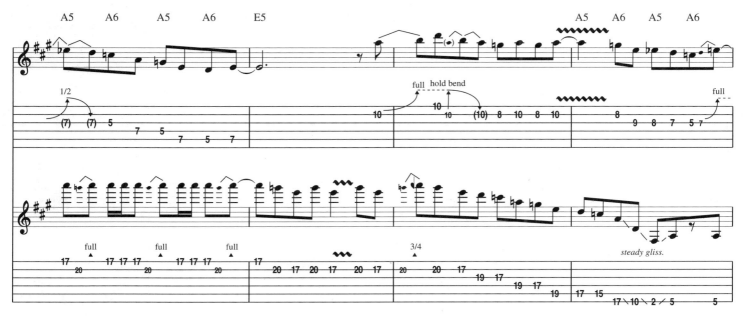

165

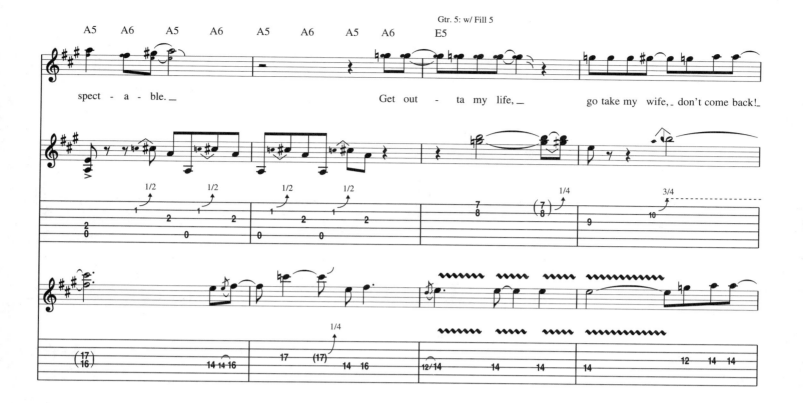

spect - a - ble. ___   Get out - ta my life, ___   go take my wife,_ don't come back!_

___   Whoo!   Ah.   A   get out - ta   my   life, ___

* Microphone fdbk. not caused by string vibration.

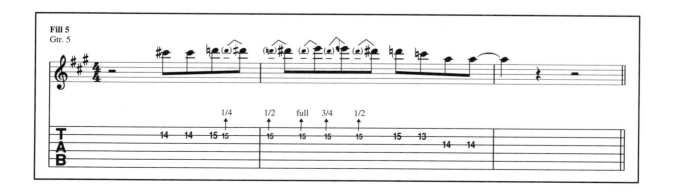

167

go take my wife,_ don't come back! _   Get out - ta my life,_

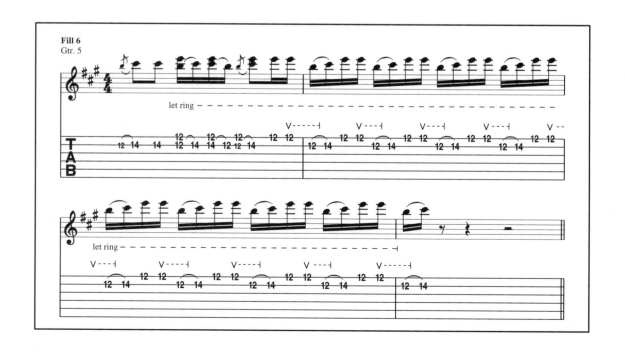

Free Time

go take my wife, _ don't come back, ___ come back! _ Ah!

* Only A (⑤ open) sustains. ** Hammer onto ⑥ and
slide to 17th fret.

169

Rocks Off

Words and Music by Mick Jagger and Keith Richards

Chorus

176

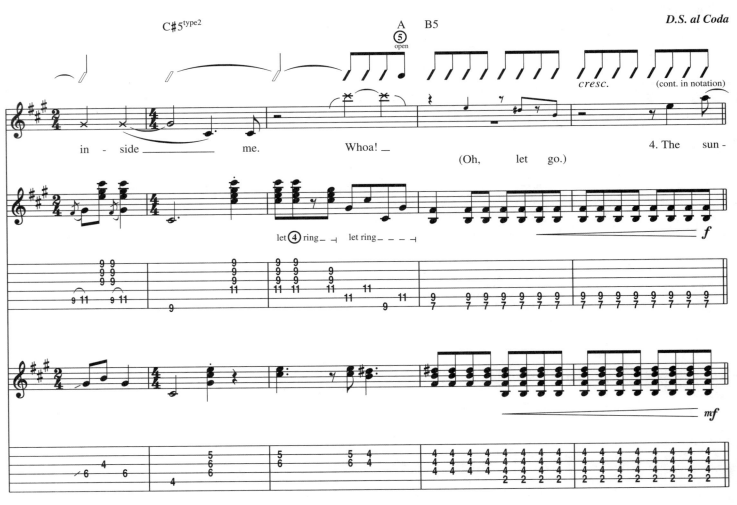

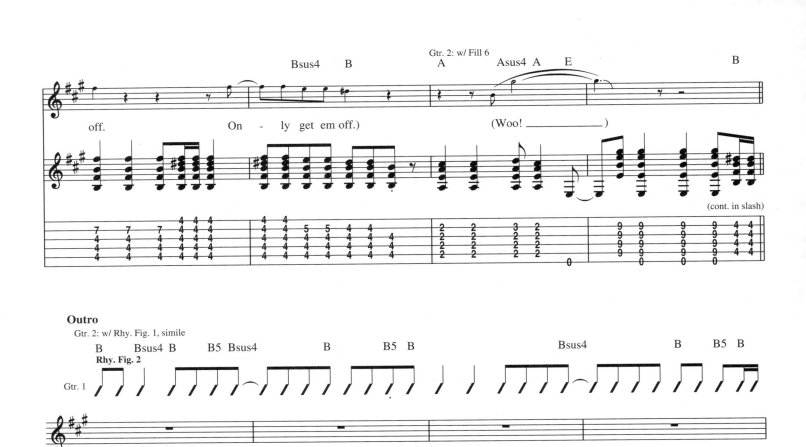

Outro

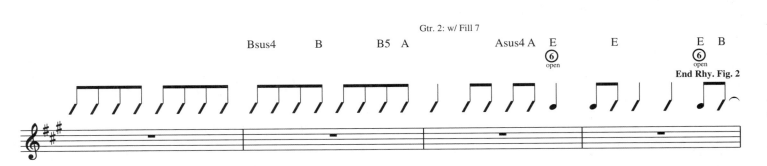

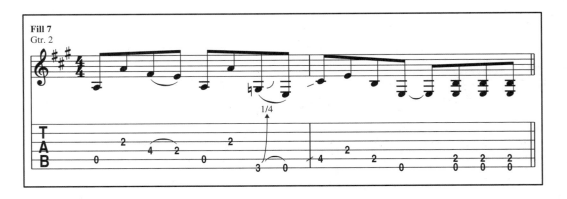

Gtr. 1: w/ Rhy. Fig. 2, 2 times, simile
Gtr. 2: w/ Rhy. Fig. 1, simile

Gtr. 3

Begin Fade

Gtr. 2: w/ Fill 3

Gtr. 2: w/ Rhy. Fig. 1, simile

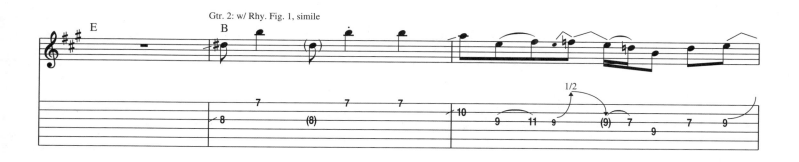

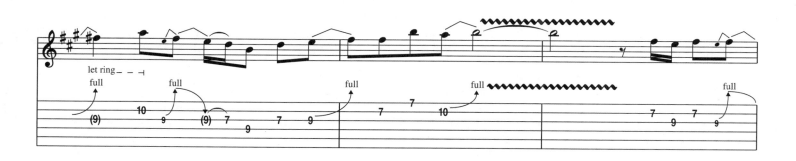

Gtr. 2: w/ Fill 3

Fade Out

Shattered

Words and Music by Mick Jagger and Keith Richards

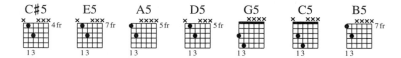

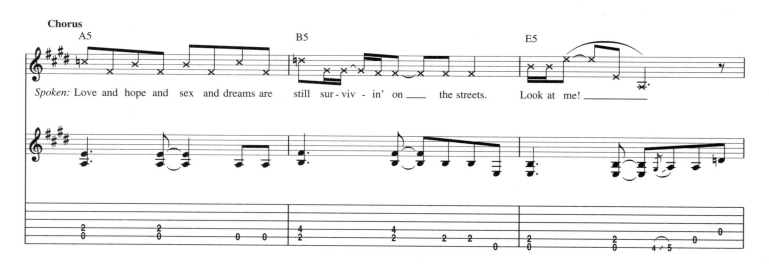

Guitar Solo

w/ Percussion Fig. 1, 8 times

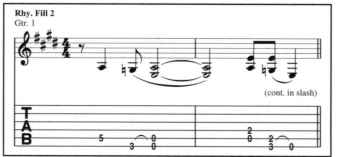

* Pedal steel arr. for elec. gtr. w/ B-string bender.

Look at me! I been shat-tered. (Shat-tered) Yeah! (Shat-tered)

Gtr. 1: w/ Rhy. Fig. 2, simile
Gtr. 7 tacet

Spoken: Pride and joy and greed and sex, that's what makes our town the best. __ Pride and joy and dir-ty dreams are

still sur-viv-in' on __ the streets and look at me! _____ I'm in tat-ters. ____
(Tat-ters.) (Shat-tered.)

She Was Hot

Words and Music by Mick Jagger and Keith Richards

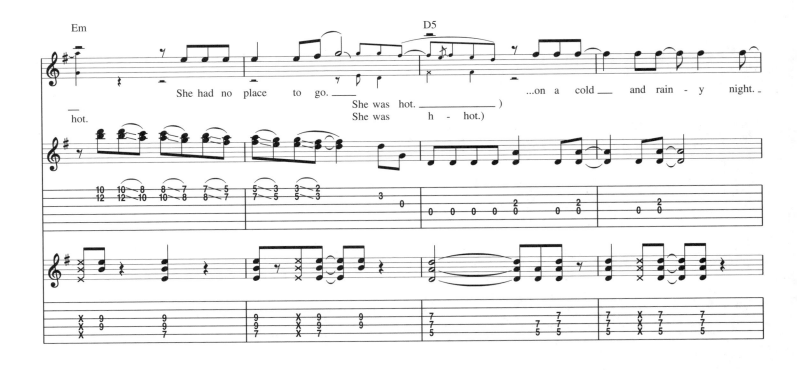

She had no place to go. ___ She was hot. ___) ...on a cold ___ and rain - y night. ___
She was hot. _____)
hot. She was h - hot.)

Guitar Solo

Whoo! _____

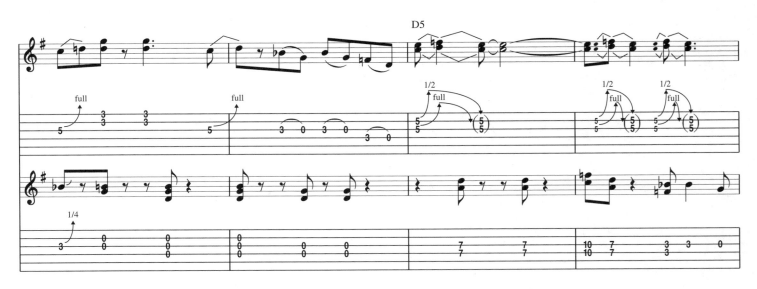

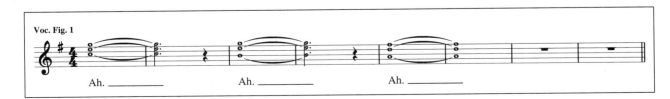

* Lead vocal is doubled (next 16 meas.)

Verse

4. Think __ I'm go - in' off __ the rails, __ rid - in' down the plea - sure trail. __ Al - ways take your pas - sion where __ you find it. __

hes - i - tate. __ (She was hot. __) She was hot.) ...on a cold __ and rain - y night. __

Hon - ey, when they're young and fresh, ____ and ____ they need the

touch of flesh, ____ go take the trea - sure where ____ you find it. ____
(Go take the trea - sure where ____ you find it.)

Chorus

And she was hot ____ in the mel - tin' snow. ____ She was hot ____ in the mol - ten glow. ____
(And she was hot. She was hot. She was hot. ____

She's So Cold

Words and Music by Mick Jagger and Keith Richards

Interlude

* Gtr. 3 is a Telecaster Fitted with a Parsons-White
   B-bender, a device which enables Ron Wood to
   bend the B string by pulling on the guitar's neck.

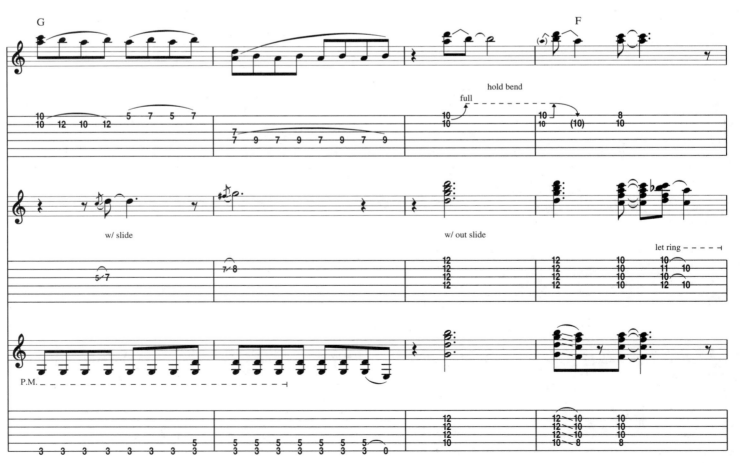

214

4. She's

Verse

so cold, she's so cold, _____ I think she was born in an arc - tic zone.

She's so cold, she's so c-c-c-cold that when I touch her my hand just froze.
(She's so cold, she's so cold.)

She's so cold, she's so god-damn cold, she's so cold, cold, cold, she's so cold. _____
(She's so cold.)

you was a beau-ty, a sweet, sweet beau-ty, a sweet, sweet beau-ty, but stone stone cold!

You're so cold, you're so cold, cold, cold. You're so cold, you're so cold. _____

(cont. in notation)

I'm so hot for you, I'm so hot for you, I'm so hot for you and you're so cold. _____

I'm the burn - in' bush, I'm the burn - in' fire, I'm the bleed - in' vol -

Start Me Up

Words and Music by Mick Jagger and Keith Richards

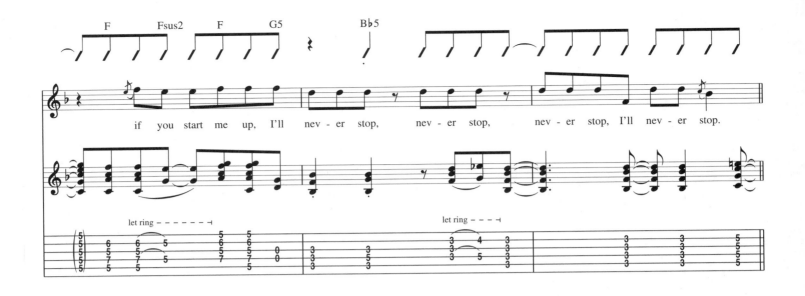

if you start me up, I'll nev-er stop, nev-er stop, nev-er stop, I'll nev-er stop.

Chorus

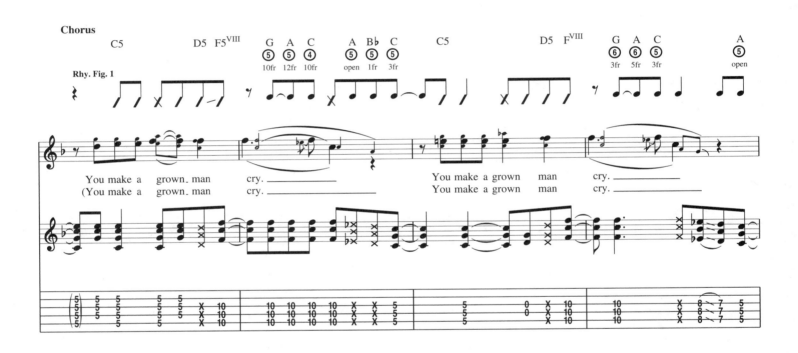

You make a grown man cry.
(You make a grown man cry.

You make a grown man cry.
You make a grown man cry.

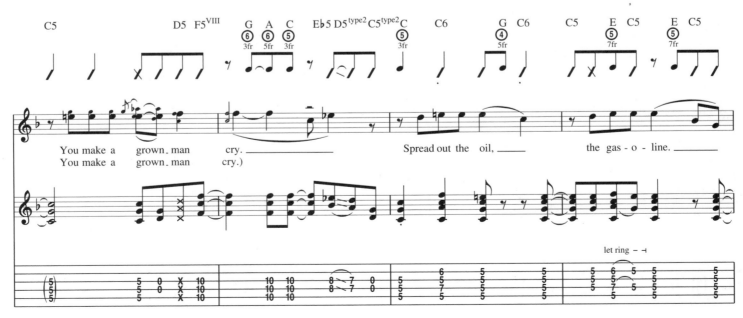

You make a grown man cry.
You make a grown man cry.)

Spread out the oil, the gas-o-line.

Chorus

Gtr. 2: w/ Rhy. Fig. 1, simile

Don't make a grown man cry. _____ Don't make a grown man cry. _____
(Don't make a grown man cry. _____ Don't make a grown man cry.

Gtr. 1

* Chord symbols reflect overall tonality.

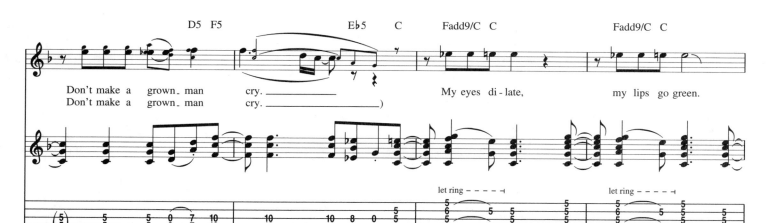

Don't make a grown man cry. _____ My eyes di-late, my lips go green.
Don't make a grown man cry. _____)

let ring - - - - ⌐   let ring - - - - ⌐

Gtr. 2: w/ Rhy. Fill 1

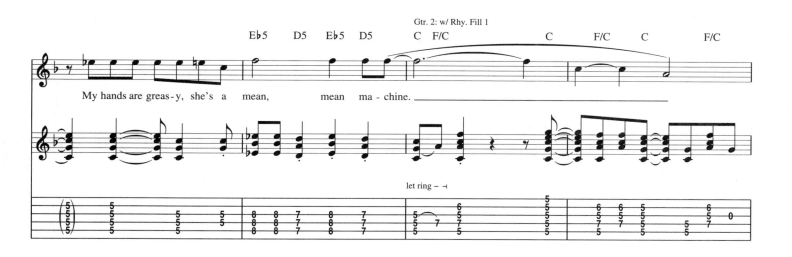

My hands are greas-y, she's a mean, mean ma-chine. _____

let ring - ⌐

Rhy. Fill 1
Gtr. 2

228

231

Time Is on My Side

Words and Music by Jerry Ragovoy

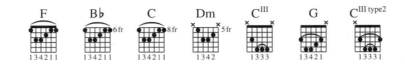

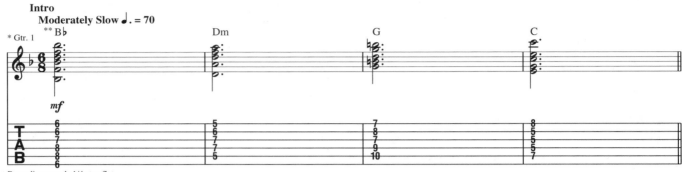

Spend the rest of my   life with you, babe.

run-ning back.   You'll   come   run-ning back   to   me._____   )

To   me._____

Interlude-Guitar Solo

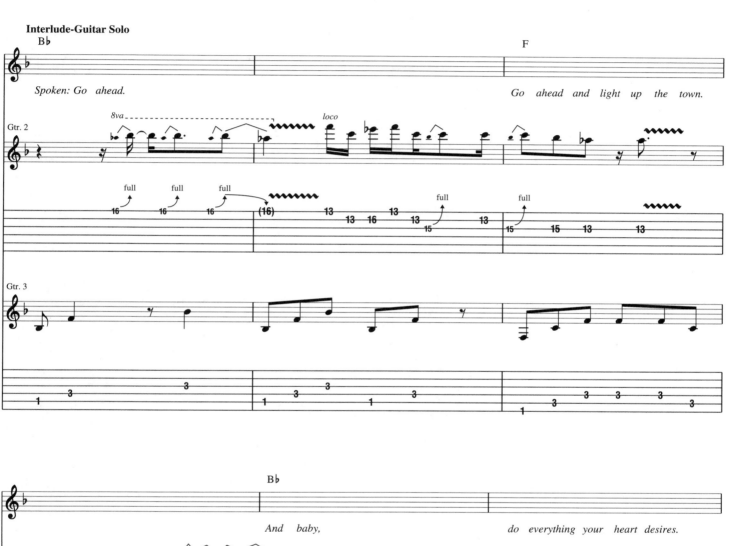

Spoken: Go ahead.

Go ahead and light up the town.

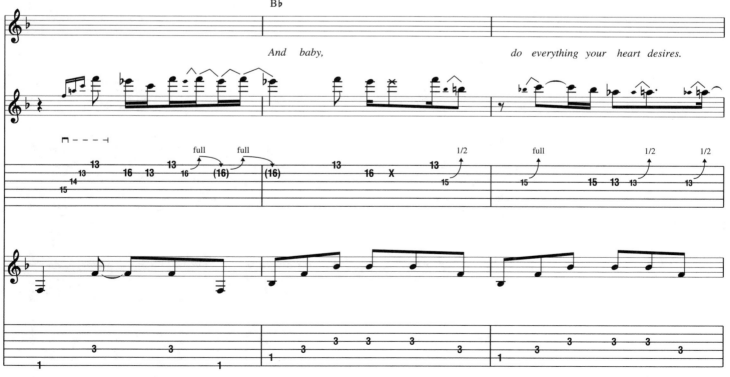

And baby,

do everything your heart desires.

Tumbling Dice

Words and Music by Mick Jagger and Keith Richards

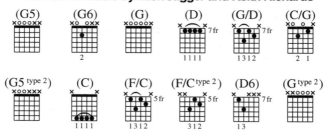

Gtrs. 1, 2, & 3:
Open G Tuning, Capo IV

① = D ④ = D
② = B ⑤ = G
③ = G ⑥ = D

Gtr. 4: Standard Tuning

Intro

Moderately ♩ = 107

Gtr. 1: w/ Rhy. Fill 1

* Strike only ④ and ⑤ whenever (G5) and (G6) are muted throughout.

† Symbols in parentheses represent chord names respective to capoed guitar when written in slash notation, and do not reflect actual sounding chords.

* Slide positioned halfway between 6th and 7th fret.

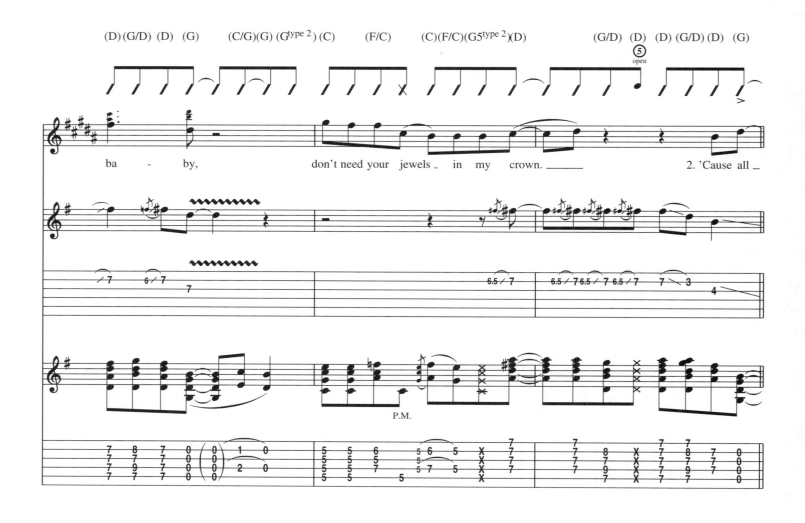

Chorus

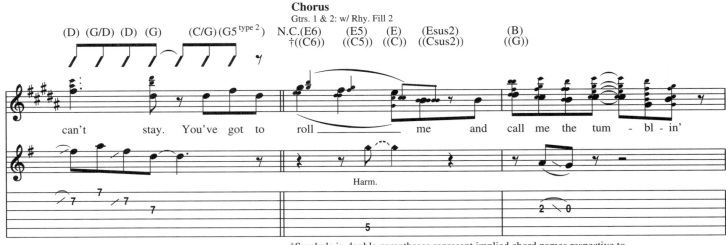

†Symbols in double parentheses represent implied chord names respective to capoed guitar. Symbols above represent actual implied chords.

Verse

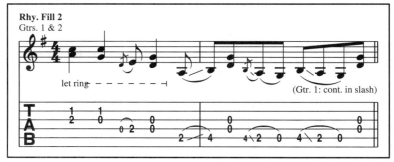

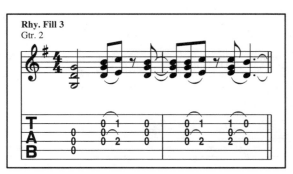

Chorus

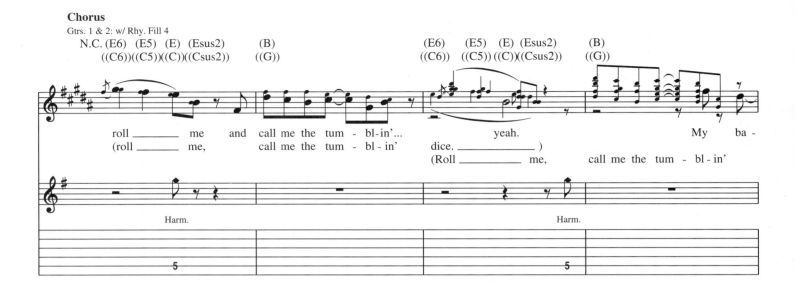

roll _____ me and call me the tum - bl-in'... yeah. My ba -
(roll _____ me, call me the tum - bl - in' dice. _____)
(Roll _____ me, call me the tum - bl - in'

Guitar Solo

- by, ooh my... yeah. ___
dice. _____)

* Gtr. & horns arr. for gtr.

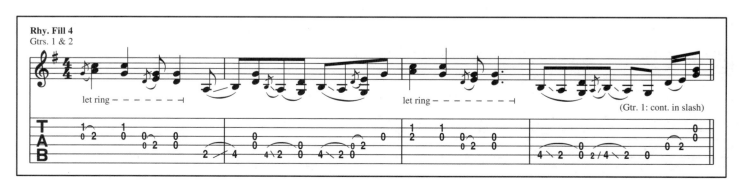

245

249

Undercover (Of the Night)

Words and Music by Mick Jagger and Keith Richards

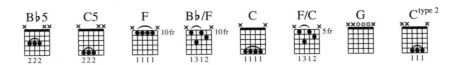

Gtrs. 1 & 3; Open G Tuning:
① = D ④ = D
② = B ⑤ = G
③ = G ⑥ = D

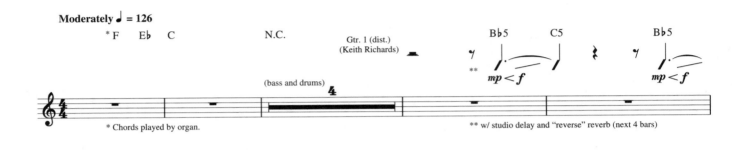

Moderately ♩ = 126

* Chords played by organ.

** w/ studio delay and "reverse" reverb (next 4 bars)

Verse

1. Hear the screams in Cen-tre For-ty-two; loud e-nough to bust your brains

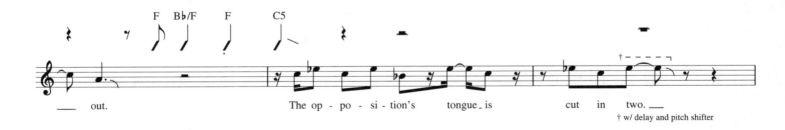

out. The op-po-si-tion's tongue is cut in two.

† w/ delay and pitch shifter

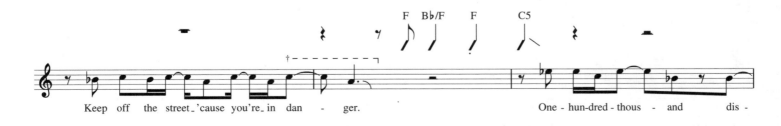

Keep off the street 'cause you're in dan-ger. One-hun-dred-thous-and dis-

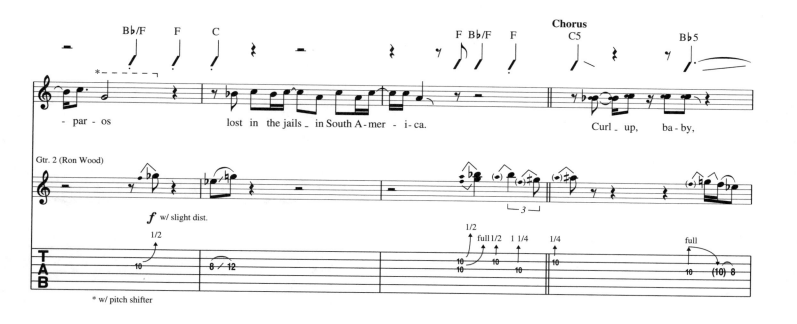

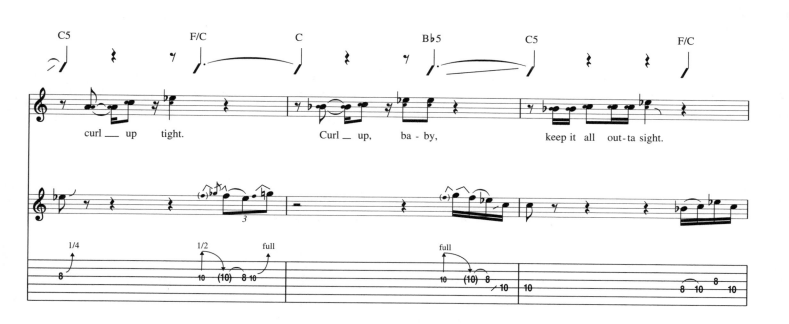

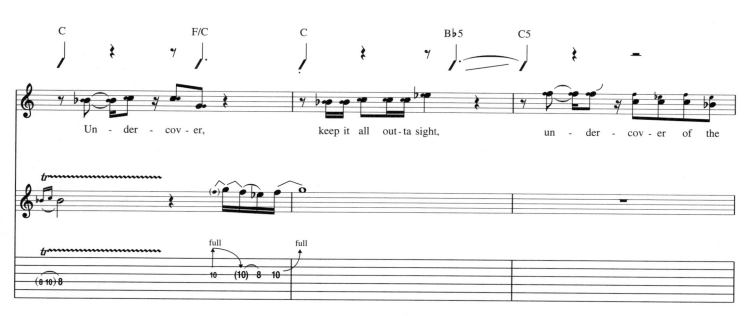

251

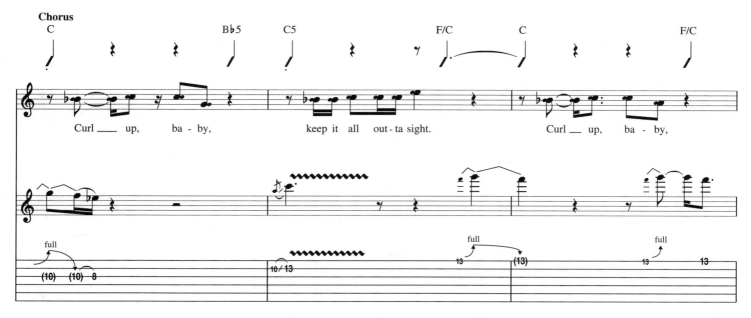

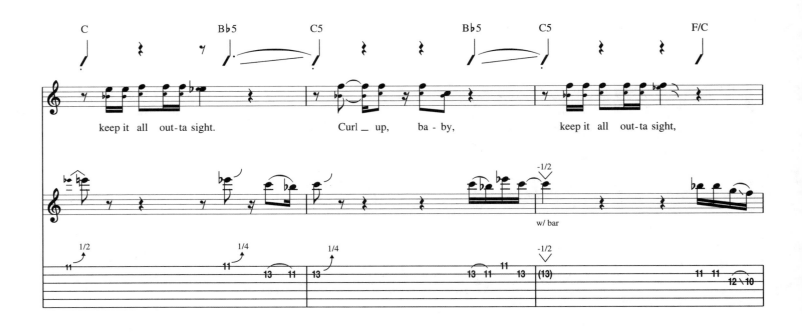

keep it all out-ta sight.   Curl __ up, ba - by,   keep it all out-ta sight,

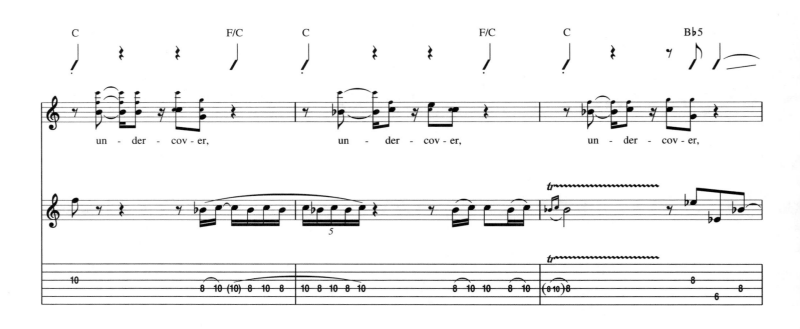

un - der - cov - er,   un - der - cov - er,   un - der - cov - er,

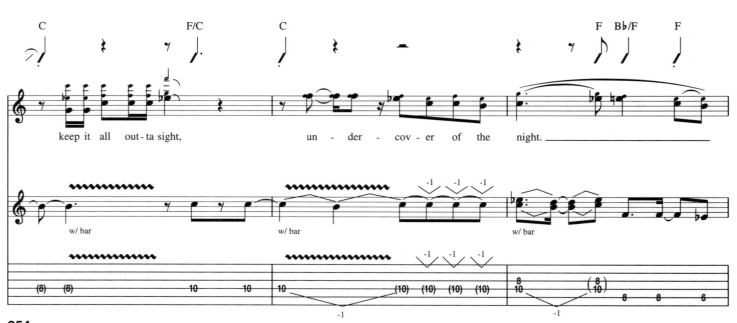

keep it all out-ta sight,   un - der - cov - er of the night. _____

Oo!   3. All the young men, they've been r - round - ed up

* w/ delay and pitch shifter

and sent to camps back in the jun - gle. 'N' peo-ple whis-per, peo-ple dou-ble talk.

Once proud fath - ers act so hum - ble. All the young girls they have got

the blues. They're head-in' on back to Cen-tre For - ty - two. Keep it

Chorus

un-der-cov-er, keep it all out-ta sight. Keep it un-der-cov-er, keep it all out-ta sight.

Un-der-cov-er, keep it all ___ out-ta sight, un-der-cov-er.
(Un-der-cov-er, all ___ out-ta sight. ___)

* w/ studio delay and "reverse" reverb (next 3 meas.)

Keep it all out-ta sight!
(out-ta sight)
Un-der-cov-er of the

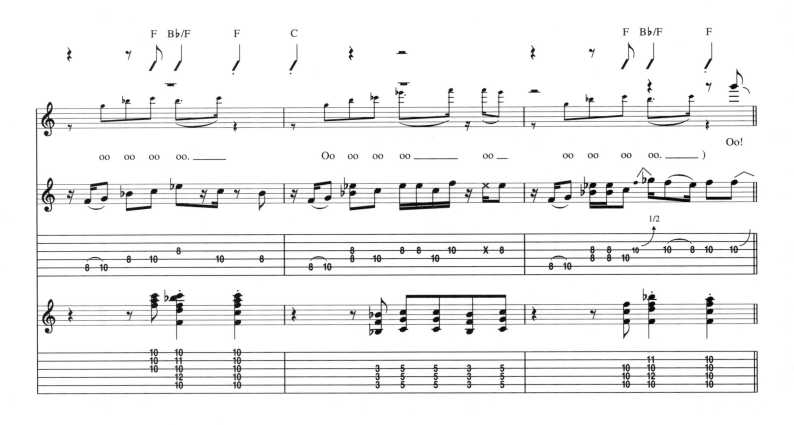

oo oo oo oo._____ Oo oo oo oo _____ oo _____ oo oo oo oo. _____) Oo!

Verse

Gtr. 3 tacet

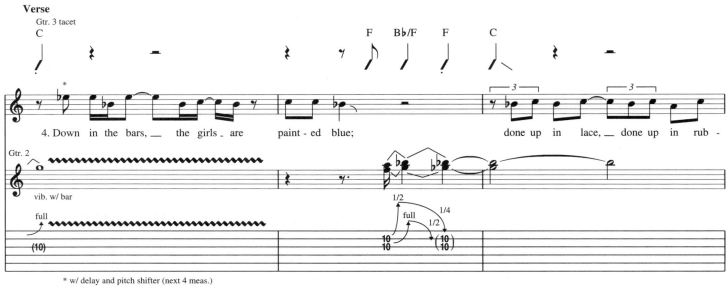

4. Down in the bars, ___ the girls ___ are paint-ed blue; ___ done up in lace, ___ done up in rub -

* w/ delay and pitch shifter (next 4 meas.)

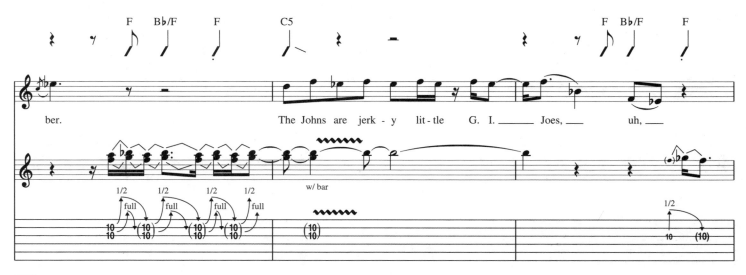

ber. The Johns are jerk - y lit - tle G. I. ___ Joes, ___ uh, ___

260

on R & R ___ from Cu-ba 'n' Rus - sia. The smell_ of sex, the smell of su - i - cide,

* w/ delay and pitch shifter (next 3 meas.)

Chorus

all these dream_things I can't keep in - side. ___ Un - der - cov - er, keep it

* w/ delay and pitch shifter

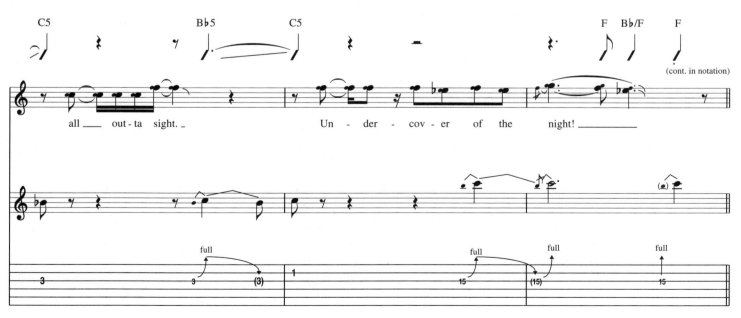

all ___ out - ta sight. _ Un - der - cov - er of the night! _____

(cont. in notation)

Outro

* w/ studio delay. Echo repeats fade out, then fade in backwards.

262

Waiting on a Friend

Words and Music by Mick Jagger and Keith Richards

*Piano arr. for gtr.

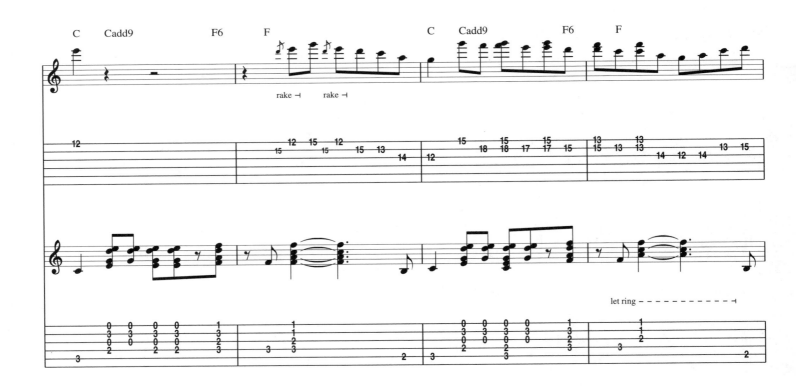

Verse

1. Watch-in' girls pas - sin' by; it ain't the lat - est thing.

Bridge

I'm ____ just stand - in' in ____ a door - way.

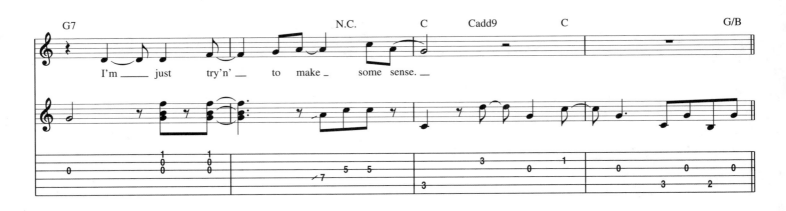

I'm ____ just try'n' ____ to make ____ some sense.

Verse

2. I love those girls that pas - sin' by, the tales they tell of men.

Chorus

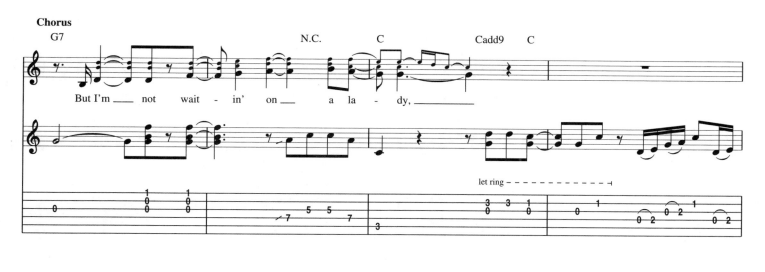

But I'm ___ not wait - in' on ___ a la - dy, ___

Chorus

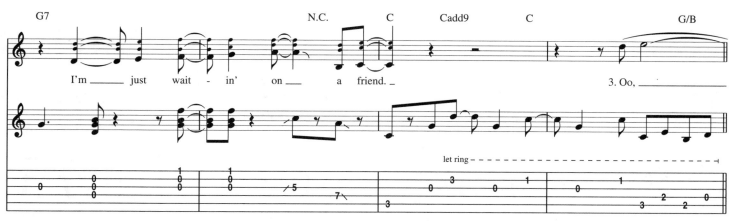

I'm ___ just wait - in' on ___ a friend. ___   3. Oo, ___

Verse

___ a smile re - lieves ___ a heart ___ that grieves; ___ re - mem - ber what I said. ___

Chorus

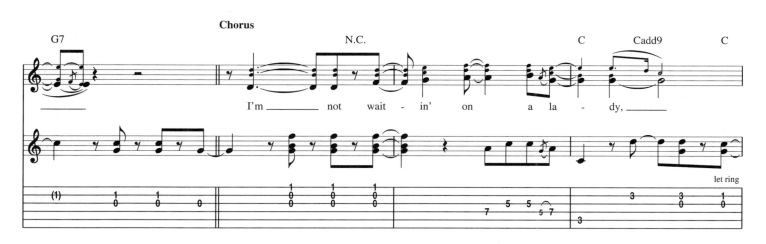

I'm ___ not wait - in' on a la - dy, ___

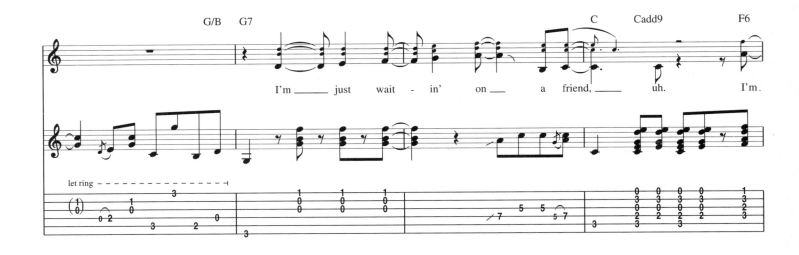

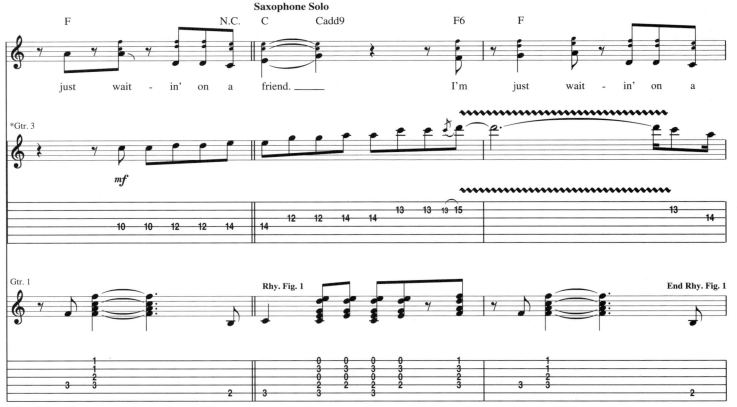

*Saxophone arr. for gtr.

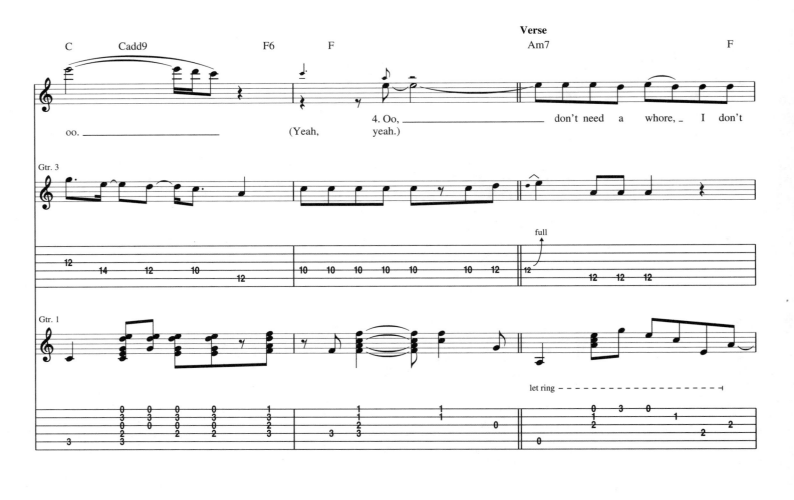

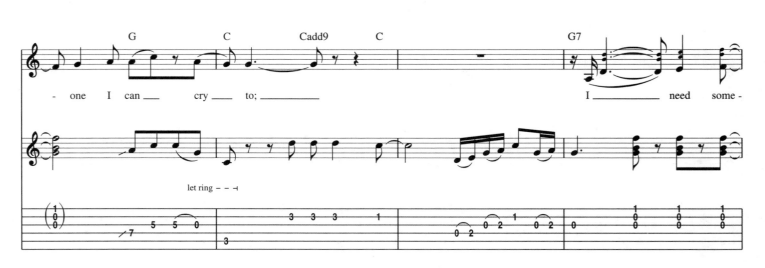

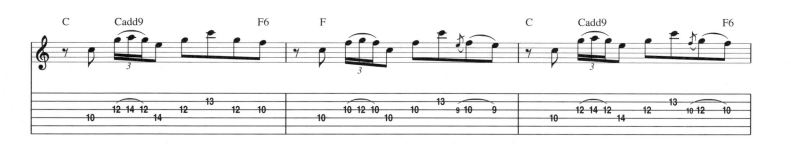

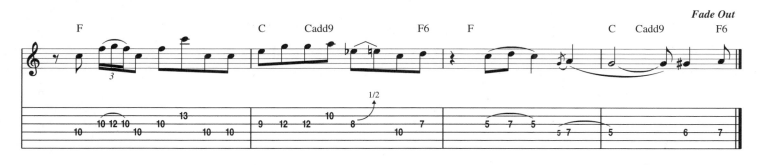

When the Whip Comes Down

Words and Music by Mick Jagger and Keith Richards

* Key signature denotes A Mixolydian.

2. Yeah, I

Verse

go to Fif-ty-third_ Street and they spit in my face, but I'm learn-in' the ropes, yeah, I'm learn-in' a trade._ Them

East Riv-er truck-ers are churn-in' the trash. _ I get so much mon-ey, but I spend it so fast. _ When the
(When the

Chorus

whip comes down. _
whip comes down. _

Yeah! _ When the whip comes down. _
When the whip comes down. _

When the
When the

I nev-er — roll ——— at all — and I nev-er cheat. An' I'm fill-in' the need, yeah, I'm

plug-gin' a hole. _ 'N' Ma - ma's _ so glad I ain't on the dole, no. When the
(When the

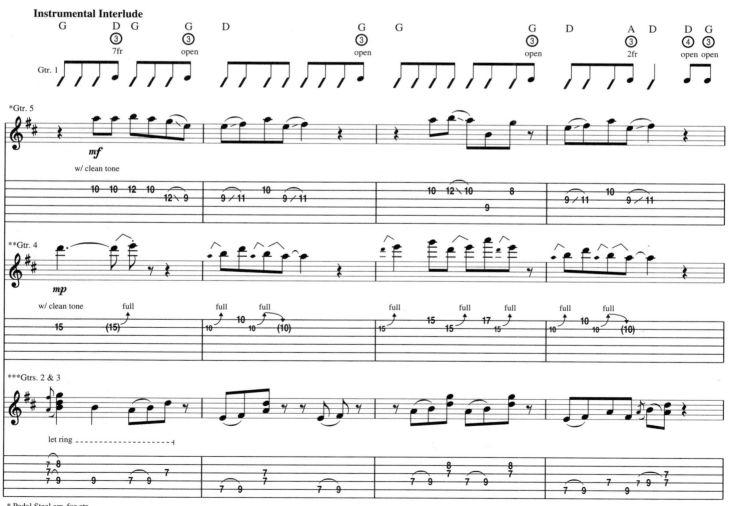

* Pedal Steel arr. for gtr.
** Gtr. 4 is a Telecaster fitted with a Parsons-White B-string Bender, a device which allows Ron Wood to bend the B-string without having to do it with his fingers.
*** Arr. for one gtr. (next 5 meas.)

whip comes down. ___
whip comes   down. _)

Yeah,   go a-head,_ jump up!

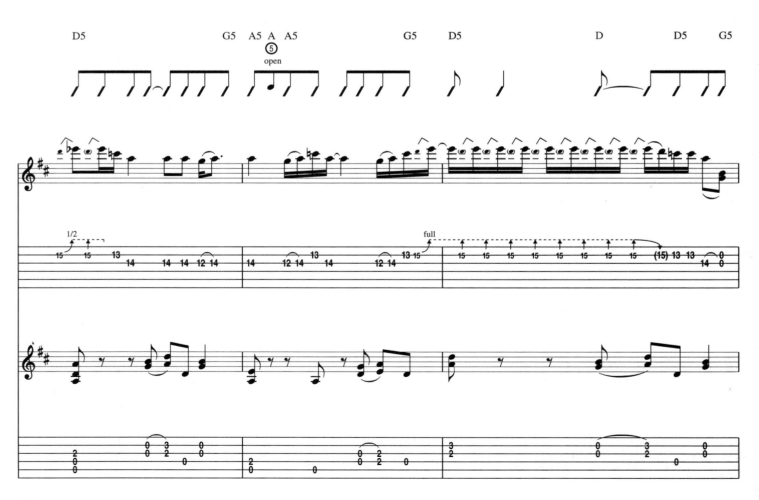

287

288

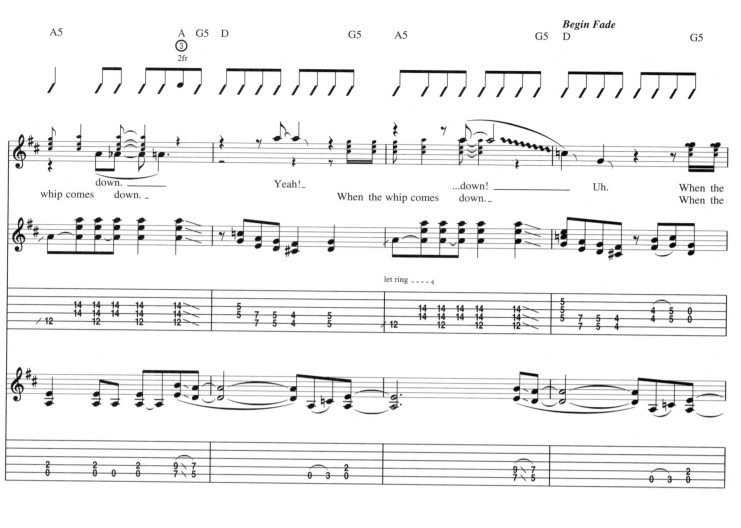

Worried About You

Words and Music by Mick Jagger and Keith Richards

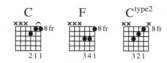

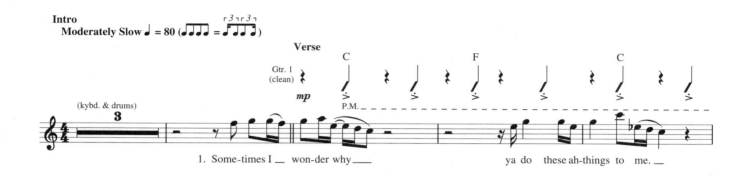

Intro
Moderately Slow ♩ = 80

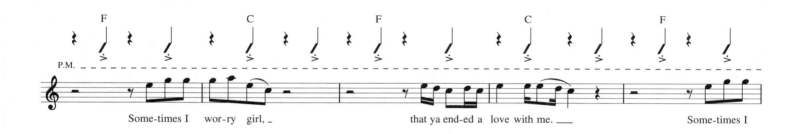

1. Some-times I __ won-der why __ ya do these ah-things to me. __

Some-times I wor-ry girl, __ that ya end-ed a love with me. __ Some-times I

see you at night. Yeah, __ I had-n't thought; __ yes, I guess you __

know by now __ that ya ain't the on - ly one. __ Yeah, _____ uh,

ba - by,＿ ooh, the sweet things that ya prom-ised me,＿ yeah, they seem just to

Gtr. 2: w/ Fill 1, 3 1/2 times

go up in smoke. Yeah, van-ish like a dream.＿ Ba - by, I

Gtr. 2: w/ Fill 2

won-der why,＿ yeah, you do these things ＿ to ＿ me. 'Cause I'm

Fill 1
Gtr. 2 (clean)

Fill 2
Gtr. 2

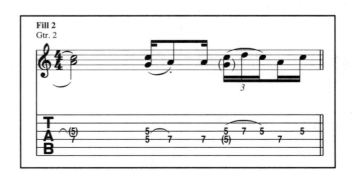

Gtr. 1: w/ Rhy. Fig. 1, 2 times, simile

love. _____ Why'd ya do it girl? I won-der why, _____ why ___ you do these

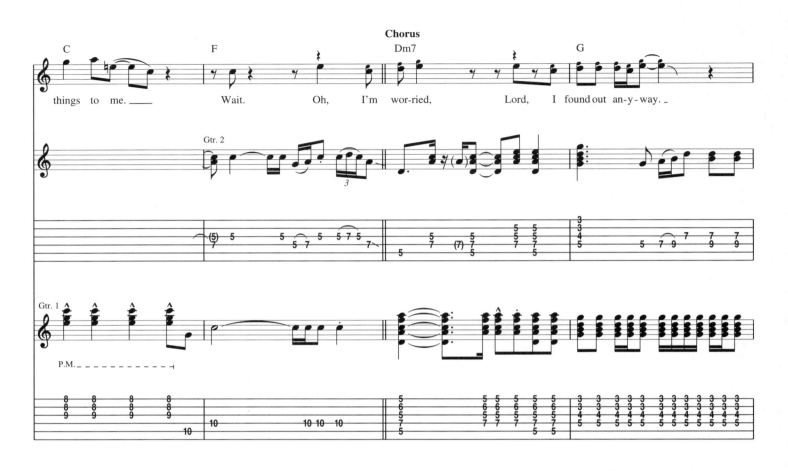

Chorus

things to me. ___ Wait. Oh, I'm wor-ried, Lord, I found out an-y-way. _

Shown _ all by _ my - self, _ and gone some day. _ See ya la-ter. I'm wor-ried, yeah, I

just can't seem to find my way. _____ Ooh. _____

Guitar Solo

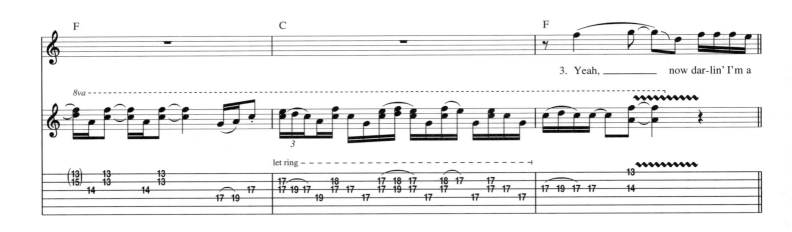

3. Yeah, _____ now dar-lin' I'm a

Verse

hard work-in' man. _____   When   did I _____   ev-er do you wrong? _____

Rhy. Fill 1
Gtr. 1

Ya got all my mon-ey ba - by, ___ yeah. ___ Ya'll . bring it, a-bring it on

home, __ yeah, I'm tell-in' the truth. Yeah, _ I want your sweet things, _ a-sweet things, ___

Lord, _____ now, that ya pro-mised me. _____ Well, I'm ___

Rhy. Fill 2
Gtr. 1

Chorus

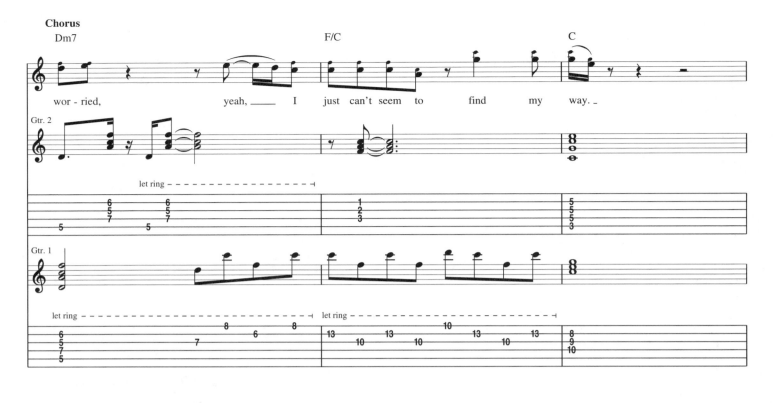

wor - ried, yeah, ___ I just can't seem to find my way. ___

Interlude

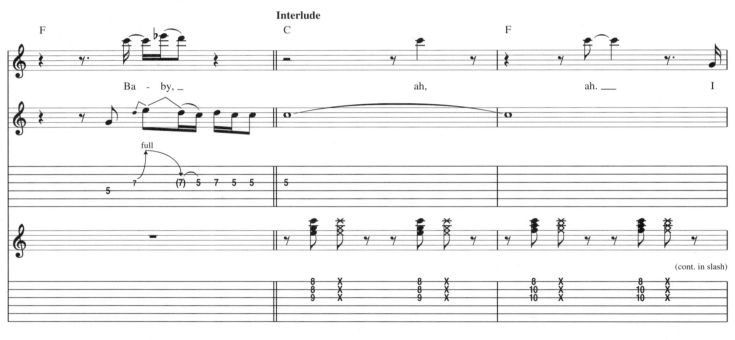

Ba - by, ___ ah, ah. ___ I

(cont. in slash)

wor-ry 'bout you, ___ yeah. ___ I wor-ry 'bout you, ___ yeah. ___

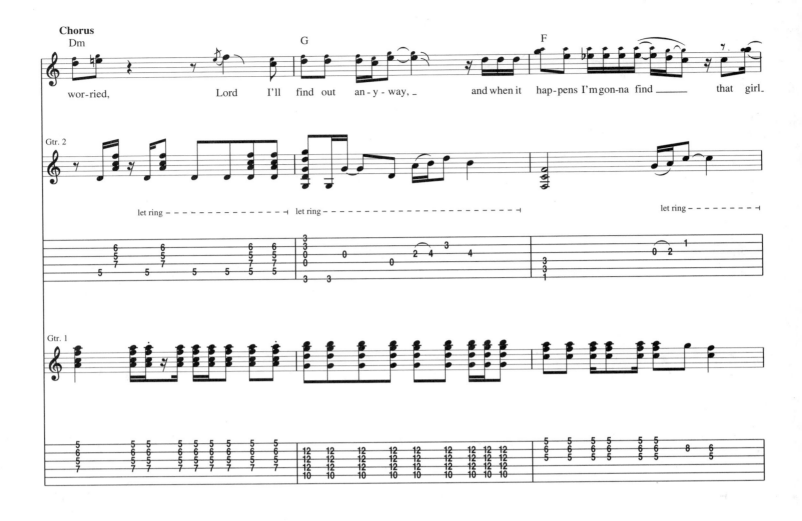

Guitar Notation Legend

Guitar Music can be notated three different ways: on a *musical staff*, in *tablature*, and in *rhythm slashes*.

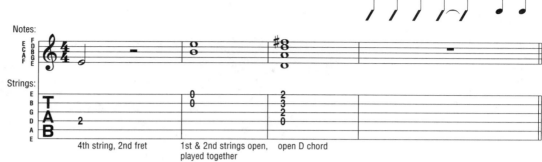

RHYTHM SLASHES are written above the staff. Strum chords in the rhythm indicated. Use the chord diagrams found at the top of the first page of the transcription for the appropriate chord voicings. Round noteheads indicate single notes.

THE MUSICAL STAFF shows pitches and rhythms and is divided by bar lines into measures. Pitches are named after the first seven letters of the alphabet.

TABLATURE graphically represents the guitar fingerboard. Each horizontal line represents a string, and each number represents a fret.

4th string, 2nd fret — 1st & 2nd strings open, played together — open D chord

HALF-STEP BEND: Strike the note and bend up 1/2 step.

WHOLE-STEP BEND: Strike the note and bend up one step.

GRACE NOTE BEND: Strike the note and bend up as indicated. The first note does not take up any time.

SLIGHT (MICROTONE) BEND: Strike the note and bend up 1/4 step.

BEND AND RELEASE: Strike the note and bend up as indicated, then release back to the original note. Only the first note is struck.

PRE-BEND: Bend the note as indicated, then strike it.

VIBRATO: The string is vibrated by rapidly bending and releasing the note with the fretting hand.

WIDE VIBRATO: The pitch is varied to a greater degree by vibrating with the fretting hand.

HAMMER-ON: Strike the first (lower) note with one finger, then sound the higher note (on the same string) with another finger by fretting it without picking.

PULL-OFF: Place both fingers on the notes to be sounded. Strike the first note and without picking, pull the finger off to sound the second (lower) note.

LEGATO SLIDE: Strike the first note and then slide the same fret-hand finger up or down to the second note. The second note is not struck.

SHIFT SLIDE: Same as legato slide, except the second note is struck.

TRILL: Very rapidly alternate between the notes indicated by continuously hammering on and pulling off.

TAPPING: Hammer ("tap") the fret indicated with the pick-hand index or middle finger and pull off to the note fretted by the fret hand.

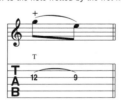

NATURAL HARMONIC: Strike the note while the fret-hand lightly touches the string directly over the fret indicated.

PINCH HARMONIC: The note is fretted normally and a harmonic is produced by adding the edge of the thumb or the tip of the index finger of the pick hand to the normal pick attack.

PICK SCRAPE: The edge of the pick is rubbed down (or up) the string, producing a scratchy sound.

MUFFLED STRINGS: A percussive sound is produced by laying the fret hand across the string(s) without depressing, and striking them with the pick hand.

PALM MUTING: The note is partially muted by the pick hand lightly touching the string(s) just before the bridge.

RAKE: Drag the pick across the strings indicated with a single motion.

TREMOLO PICKING: The note is picked as rapidly and continuously as possible.

VIBRATO BAR DIVE AND RETURN: The pitch of the note or chord is dropped a specified number of steps (in rhythm) then returned to the original pitch.

VIBRATO BAR SCOOP: Depress the bar just before striking the note, then quickly release the bar.

VIBRATO BAR DIP: Strike the note and then immediately drop a specified number of steps, then release back to the original pitch.

RECORDED VERSIONS

The Best Note-For-Note Transcriptions Available

ALL BOOKS INCLUDE TABLATURE

00690501 Adams, Bryan – Greatest Hits $19.95	00690323 Fastball – All the Pain Money Can Buy $19.95	00690546 P.O.D. – Satellite . . . .$19.
00692015 Aerosmith – Greatest Hits $22.95	00690235 Foo Fighters – The Colour and the Shape .$19.95	00693864 Police, The – Best of . . . .$19.
00690488 Aerosmith – Just Push Play $19.95	00690394 Foo Fighters –	00690299 Presley, Elvis – Best of Elvis:
00690178 Alice in Chains – Acoustic $19.95	There Is Nothing Left to Lose $19.95	The King of Rock 'n' Roll . . . .$19.
00690387 Alice in Chains – Nothing Safe –	00690222 G3 Live – Satriani, Vai, Johnson $22.95	00694975 Queen – Greatest Hits . . . .$24.
The Best of the Box $19.95	00690536 Garbage – Beautiful Garbage $19.95	00694910 Rage Against the Machine . . . .$19.
00694932 Allman Brothers Band – Volume 1 . . . . .$24.95	00690438 Genesis Guitar Anthology $19.95	00690145 Rage Against the Machine – Evil Empire .$19.
00694933 Allman Brothers Band – Volume 2 . . . . .$24.95	00690338 Goo Goo Dolls – Dizzy Up the Girl $19.95	00694978 Rage Against the Machine – Renegades . .$19.
00690513 American Hi-Fi $19.95	00690576 Goo Goo Dolls – Gutterflower $19.95	00690426 Ratt – Best of . . . .$19.
00694878 Atkins, Chet – Vintage Fingerstyle $19.95	00690114 Guy, Buddy – Collection Vol. A-J $22.95	00690055 Red Hot Chili Peppers –
00690418 Audio Adrenaline, Best of $17.95	00690193 Guy, Buddy – Collection Vol. L-Y $22.95	Bloodsugarsexmagik . . . .$19.
00690366 Bad Company Original Anthology - Bk 1 .$19.95	00694798 Harrison, George – Anthology $19.95	00690584 Red Hot Chili Peppers – By the Way . . . .$19.
00690367 Bad Company Original Anthology - Bk 2 .$19.95	00692930 Hendrix, Jimi – Are You Experienced? $24.95	00690379 Red Hot Chili Peppers – Californication . .$19.
00690503 Beach Boys – Very Best of $19.95	00692931 Hendrix, Jimi – Axis: Bold As Love $22.95	00690090 Red Hot Chili Peppers – One Hot Minute .$22.
00690489 Beatles – 1 . . . .$24.95	00690017 Hendrix, Jimi – Woodstock $24.95	00694899 R.E.M. – Automatic for the People . . . . .$19.
00694929 Beatles – 1962-1966 . . . .$24.95	00660029 Holly, Buddy $19.95	00690511 Reinhardt, Django – Definitive Collection .$19.
00694930 Beatles – 1967-1970 . . . .$24.95	00690457 Incubus – Make Yourself $19.95	00690014 Rolling Stones – Exile on Main Street . . .$24.
00694832 Beatles – For Acoustic Guitar $19.95	00690544 Incubus – Morningview $19.95	00690031 Santana's Greatest Hits . . . .$19.
00690503 Beatles – Hard Day's Night $16.95	00690136 Indigo Girls – 1200 Curfews $22.95	00690566 Scorpions – Best of . . . .$19.
00690482 Beatles – Let It Be $16.95	00690457 Joel, Billy – For Guitar $19.95	00120123 Shepherd, Kenny Wayne – Trouble Is . . .$19.
00694884 Benson, George – Best of $19.95	00694912 Johnson, Eric – Ah Via Musicom $19.95	00690419 Slipknot . . . .$19.
00692385 Berry, Chuck $19.95	00690271 Johnson, Robert – The New Transcriptions .$24.95	00690530 Slipknot – Iowa . . . .$19.
00692200 Black Sabbath –	00699131 Joplin, Janis – Best of $19.95	00690385 Sonicflood . . . .$19.
We Sold Our Soul for Rock 'N' Roll $19.95	00693185 Judas Priest – Vintage Hits $19.95	00694957 Stewart, Rod – Unplugged...And Seated . .$22.
00690305 Blink 182 – Dude Ranch $19.95	00690504 King, Albert – The Very Best of $19.95	00690021 Sting – Fields of Gold . . . .$19.
00690389 Blink 182 – Enema of the State $19.95	00690444 King, B.B. and Eric Clapton –	00690520 Styx Guitar Collection . . . .$19.
00690523 Blink 182 – Take Off Your Pants & Jacket .$19.95	Riding with the King $19.95	00690519 Sum 41 – All Killer No Filler . . . .$19.
00690028 Blue Oyster Cult – Cult Classics $19.95	00690339 Kinks, The – Best of $19.95	00690425 System of a Down . . . .$19.
00690583 Boxcar Racer $19.95	00690279 Liebert, Ottmar + Luna Negra –	00690531 System of a Down – Toxicity . . . .$19.
00690491 Bowie, David – Best of $19.95	Opium Highlights $19.95	00694824 Taylor, James – Best of $16
00690451 Buckley, Jeff – Collection $24.95	00690525 Lynch, George – Best of $19.95	00690238 Third Eye Blind . . . .$19.
00690364 Cake – Songbook $19.95	00694755 Malmsteen, Yngwie – Rising Force $19.95	00690580 311 – From Chaos . . . .$19.
00690565 Calling, The – Camino Palmero $29.95	00694956 Marley, Bob – Legend $19.95	00690295 Tool – Aenima . . . .$19.
00690293 Chapman, Steven Curtis – Best of $19.95	00690548 Marley, Bob – One Love: Very Best of $19.95	00690039 Vai, Steve – Alien Love Secrets . . . .$24.
00690043 Cheap Trick – Best of $19.95	00694945 Marley, Bob – Songs of Freedom $24.95	00690343 Vai, Steve – Flex-able Leftovers . . . .$19.
00690171 Chicago – Definitive Guitar Collection . . .$22.95	00690382 McLachlan, Sarah – Mirrorball $19.95	00690392 Vai, Steve – The Ultra Zone . . . .$19.
00690590 Clapton, Eric – Anthology $29.95	00690239 Matchbox 20 – Yourself or Someone Like You .$19.95	00690370 Vaughan, Stevie Ray and Double Trouble –
00692931 Clapton, Eric – Best of, 2nd Edition $22.95	00694952 Megadeth – Countdown to Extinction $19.95	The Real Deal: Greatest Hits Volume 2 . . .$22
00690415 Clapton Chronicles – Best of Eric Clapton .$18.95	00694951 Megadeth – Rust in Peace $22.95	00690116 Vaughan, Stevie Ray – Guitar Collection . .$24
00690074 Clapton, Eric – The Cream of Clapton $24.95	00690495 Megadeth – The World Needs a Hero $19.95	00660058 Vaughan, Stevie Ray –
00694869 Clapton, Eric – Unplugged $22.95	00690505 Mellencamp, John – Guitar Collection . . .$19.95	Lightnin' Blues 1983-1987 . . . .$24
00690162 Clash, Best of The $19.95	00690448 MxPx – The Ever Passing Moment $19.95	00690550 Vaughan, Stevie Ray and Double Trouble –
00690494 Coldplay – Parachutes $19.95	00690500 Nelson, Ricky – Guitar Collection $17.95	Live at Montreux 1982 & 1985 . . . . . .$24
00690593 Coldplay – A Rush of Blood to the Head . .$19.95	00690189 Nirvana – From the Muddy	00694835 Vaughan, Stevie Ray – The Sky Is Crying . .$22.
00690306 Coryell, Larry – Collection $19.95	Banks of the Wishkah $19.95	00690015 Vaughan, Stevie Ray – Texas Flood $19
00694940 Counting Crows – August & Everything After .$19.95	00694913 Nirvana – In Utero $19.95	00694789 Waters, Muddy – Deep Blues . . . .$24.
00694840 Cream – Disraeli Gears $19.95	00694883 Nirvana – Nevermind™ $19.95	00690071 Weezer (The Blue Album) $19
00690401 Creed – Human Clay $19.95	00690026 Nirvana – Unplugged in New York $19.95	00690516 Weezer (The Green Album) . . . .$19.
00690352 Creed – My Own Prison $19.95	00690121 Oasis – (What's the Story) Morning Glory . .$19.95	00690579 Weezer – Maladroit . . . .$19.
00690551 Creed – Weathered $19.95	00690358 Offspring, The – Americana $19.95	00690286 Weezer – Pinkerton $19
00699521 Cure, The $24.95	00690485 Offspring, The – Conspiracy of One $19.95	00690447 Who, The – Best of . . . .$24.
00690484 dc Talk – Intermission: The Greatest Hits .$19.95	00690552 Offspring, The – Ignition $19.95	00690320 Williams, Dar – Best of $17
00690289 Deep Purple, Best of $17.95	00694847 Osbourne, Ozzy – Best of $22.95	00690319 Wonder, Stevie – Some of the Best . . . . . .$17.
00690563 Default – The Fallout $19.95	00690547 Osbourne, Ozzy – Down to Earth $19.95	00690443 Zappa, Frank – Hot Rats $19
00690384 Di Franco, Ani – Best of $19.95	00690399 Osbourne, Ozzy – Ozzman Cometh $19.95	00690589 ZZ Top Guitar Anthology $22
00690380 Di Franco, Ani – Up Up Up Up Up Up $19.95	00690538 Oysterhead – The Grand Pecking Order . .$19.95	
00695382 Dire Straits – Sultans of Swing $19.95	00694855 Pearl Jam – Ten $19.95	
00690347 Doors, The – Anthology $22.95	00690439 Perfect Circle, A – Mer De Noms $19.95	
00690348 Doors, The – Essential Guitar Collection . .$16.95	00690499 Petty, Tom – The Definitive	
00690533 Electric Light Orchestra Guitar Collection .$19.95	Guitar Collection $19.95	
00690555 Etheridge, Melissa – Best of $19.95	00690424 Phish – Farmhouse $19.95	
00690524 Etheridge, Melissa – Skin $19.95	00690240 Phish – Hoist $19.95	
00690349 Eve 6 . . . .$19.95	00690331 Phish – Story of the Ghost $19.95	
00690496 Everclear, Best of $19.95	00690428 Pink Floyd – Dark Side of the Moon $19.95	
00690515 Extreme II – Pornograffitti $19.95	00690456 P.O.D. – The Fundamental	
	Elements of Southtown $19.95